VIRUS AS A SUMMONS TO FAITH

Also by Walter Brueggemann

VIRUS AS A SUMMONS TO FAITH

Biblical Reflections in a Time of
Loss, Grief, and Uncertainty

Walter Brueggemann

Foreword by
Nahum Ward-Lev

CASCADE *Books* • Eugene, Oregon

VIRUS AS A SUMMONS TO FAITH
Biblical Reflections in a Time of Loss, Grief, and Uncertainty

Cascade Books
An Imprint of Wipf and Stock Publishers
199 W. 8th Ave., Suite 3
Eugene, OR 97401

www.wipfandstock.com

PAPERBACK ISBN: 978–1-7252-7673-4
HARDCOVER ISBN: 978–1-7252-7674-1
EBOOK ISBN: 978–1-7252-767 5-8

Cataloging-in-Publication data:

Names: Brueggemann, Walter, author. | Ward-Lev, Nahum, foreword.

Title: Virus as a summons to faith : biblical reflections in a time of loss, grief, and uncertainty / Walter Brueggemann ; foreword by Rabbi Nahum Ward-Lev.

Description: Eugene, OR : Cascade Books, 2020. | Includes bibliographical references and index.

Identifiers: ISBN: 978–1-7252-7673-4 (PAPERBACK). | ISBN: 978–1-7252-7674-1 (HARDCOVER). | ISBN: 978–1-7252-767 5-8 (EBOOK).

Subjects: LCSH: Bible—Old Testament—Criticism, interpretation, etc. | Bible—Theology. | Bible—Old Testament—Homiletical use.

Classification: BV4211.3 B773 2020 (print). | BV4211.3 (epub).

Manufactured in the U.S.A.   MAY 8, 2020

CONTENTS

FOREWORD

O nly Walter Brueggemann could have written this book. Most people in the United States have been grappling with the severity of the Covid-19 crisis for about six weeks. In this short time, Professor Brueggemann has written a profound, insightful, and actionable book, bringing forth deep biblical wisdom to provide real support and guidance to face the present crisis.

Professor Brueggemann has long been a profound source of biblical wisdom. For over two generations, he has brilliantly brought forth the insights of those ancient Scriptures to meet contemporary issues and challenges. His thin volume that you hold in your hand is an invaluable source of guidance—spiritual, psychological, social, and political—for how we can bring new life out of the death and destruction we find all around us.

As a rabbi and a lifelong student of the Hebrew Scriptures, I find biblical wisdom speaking into the present moment with more relevance and power than at any other time in my life. At this critical moment, many people are sitting with the stark awareness that the world we knew is gone. There is no going back. Humankind faces a pressing and daunting learning challenge. We are called to learn how to peaceably relinquish the old world and how to imaginatively give birth to a new world in which all life can flourish. Seeking wisdom for the learning journey ahead of us, I find myself repeatedly turning to the Hebrew Bible. These Scriptures, the Torah and the Prophets in particular, were gathered and edited to meet the needs of the Israelite people who had suffered the catastrophe of the Babylonian destruction and subsequent exile in the sixth century BCE. These writings were held sacred because they helped people absorb the loss of the world they had known and offered a vision for a way forward. These writings can provide vital insights to help us meet the challenges of the disaster in our day. Brueggemann's new and timely book is a rich exploration of these invaluable ancient insights.

In *Virus as a Summons to Faith*, the summons that Professor Brueggemann hears in the devastation caused by the Covid-19 virus is the same summons that all prophets hear in the midst of calamity: the call into right relationship with Living Presence, a call into deeper, more caring, and mutually beneficial relationship with all that is. In the biblical language that has long been at the core of Brueggemann's thinking, the devastating effects of the virus summon us to renew our covenantal relationship with God and to renew our responsibilities within that relationship.

Professor Brueggemann's discussion of covenantal relationship opens up a powerful exploration about how humankind can live through this disaster toward a more fruitful and inclusive future. I was moved to find in his writings a God whose mercy is present even amid the disaster. I was heartened to meet a God whose tenacious, unrelenting solidarity with humankind supports the human yearning to grow toward love, generosity, and hospitality—even or especially in the midst of a calamity. Brueggemann's understanding of a merciful God in steadfast solidarity with humankind has become for me a strong and abiding basis for hope and action in the face of the pandemic.

I found the chapter "Praying amid the Virus" particularly helpful for my prayer life. Brueggemann sets forth prayer as the primary way a person deepens covenantal awareness and attentiveness. In prayer we embody and enact a trusting relationship. Through prayer we grow in awareness of God's mercy and God's steadfast solidarity. The expectation of prayer, then, is not that a given request be granted but rather that a covenantal relationship be enacted and trusted, a relationship that in itself "recontextualizes the disaster."

Brueggemann's meditation on Psalm 77 takes us to the heart of the matter. He focuses on the turn we are summoned to make in the face of the current calamity, the turn from the small, preoccupied self to the larger Self we find in God. For Brueggemann, this turn toward the mysterious and unknowable Thou liberates humankind to take bold and imaginative action toward a world of neighborliness, a community of care and generosity for one's neighbor.

Brueggemann's concluding two chapters are a call to birth a new future. The virus has lain bare what people who have been oppressed or marginalized have long known—the injustice and unsustainability of the old order. In these chapters, Brueggemann brings us Isaiah's promise that God is doing "a new thing," a promise that summons humankind to radical, prophetic imaginings and actions toward a new and flourishing world.

Alongside Isaiah's bright promise, Brueggemann brings us the prophet's surprising and evocative vision of God groaning and gasping like a woman in labor. Radical newness is not pain-free for God. Brueggemann learns from Isaiah that such birthing will not be free of pain for us. A new world will come with a cost. The price of newness is the full acknowledgment that the old creation has failed and therefore must be relinquished, renounced, and repented. Such letting go is painful. Nevertheless, we are summoned to this relinquishing and to this birthing. Brueggemann teaches us that our covenant with Living Presence summons us to meet our covenantal responsibility and, at the same time, gifts us with God's mercy and tenacious solidarity, a steadfast love that is strong enough to see us through.

I want to conclude with expressing the deep honor I feel, as Walter's long-time student, in writing the foreword for his current book. The opportunity to write this foreword came out of a relationship between a teacher and a student that has grown over the years. Our relationship grew out of a single letter. In 2009, the learning circle I lead was struggling with the violence that God exhibits in the Hebrew Bible. As a devoted reader of Professor Brueggemann's books, I wanted to know what he thought about

God's violence. To my delight, soon after I sent my letter, I received Walter's reply. His response was characteristically thoughtful, honest, and humble. Over the years, as our learning circle read more deeply into the prophets, I wrote more letters. The letters became emails and emails became telephone conversations. In time, I turned to Walter for moral and scholarly support for my own writing on the prophets. In each of these many exchanges, I found Walter to be generous with his time, brilliantly insightful, and bone-deep honest. He has been for me a great teacher about how to live Scriptures into one's life.

Through this new and important book, I am hoping that my teacher's timely teaching will reach an even broader audience than all his previous books. This book deserves that degree of attention. We can all be profoundly grateful to Professor Brueggemann for providing us with a comforting, challenging, and invaluable resource to guide us through these difficult times.

Rabbi Nahum Ward-Lev
Santa Fe, New Mexico
April 24, 2020

PREFACE

It is likely that every leader in a community of faith now faces an opportunity or a responsibility (or both) to comment on the current virus as it may be understood through the lens of critical faith. Or, conversely, to comment on how critical faith may be more poignantly understood through the lens of the current virus. The reflections I offer here are my attempt to accept that opportunity and that responsibility. It is my hope that my thinking may be of some encouragement and suggestion about how we may think and speak critically, theologically, and biblically about our current crisis of virus in order that the community of faith may maintain its missional identity with boldness and joy.

It will be seen that in every case I have given close attention to biblical texts; that is because I, as Bible teacher, believe that any serious crisis is a summons for us to reread the Bible afresh. I think that is now a summons to which we must and can respond. It can also be noticed in what follows that once I have done some close textual work, I have tried to move on to explore possible extrapolations from textual work and to identify problems that arise for us from such work.

In this season of crisis, I am aware of many colleagues in ministry who live, move, believe, and act in very difficult circumstances of ministry. This is my attempt to stand in solidarity with such colleagues and perhaps to offer resource and energy for that on-going work.

To complete this book, I have included two of my previously published pieces. First, I have included "The 'Turn' from Self to God," *The Journal for Preachers* 6 (1983) 8–14, an exposition of Psalm 77. In that Psalm the speaker turns abruptly from self-reference to the "Thou" of God. We are making that same turn amid the virus as we learn yet again about the inadequacy of the autonomous self. Second, I have included a revised version of "The Matrix of Groan," *The Journal for Preachers* 24/2 (2001) 17–23, which concerns the cruciality of out loud groans for faith. We are now, amid the virus, in such a matrix of groan about loss, fear, and death. It is clear that yet again we must wait amid that matrix of groan to receive what new good futures God may now give to us.

As always, I am grateful to K. C. Hanson and Wipf and Stock for seeing my work through to publication. And I am grateful to my friend, Rabbi Nahum Ward-Lev of Santa Fe, New Mexico, for his thoughtful foreword to the book.

I am glad to acknowledge that my initial essay, "Reaping the Whirlwind" was first published as a "Special Paper" by the *Journal of Preachers* (March 2020). It may be that Palm Sunday is an appropriate time for me to write this, as that public occasion marked the distinctive power embodied by Jesus and mediated by Jesus to his followers that bewildered the authorities (Mark 11:18). His power, unlike the power that the world most notices, is the force of transformative vulnerability and foolish wisdom. That strange power is now entrusted to his faithful community. It requires some daring effort in our current crisis for us to imagine what form that power may now take. As we do that work of imagining, we are reminded that the festal cry, "Hosanna," before it was glad acclamation, was a passionate petition, "Save us, we pray!" That strange mix of *acclamation/petition* is a proper mood in which we now do our faith most faithfully.

Walter Brueggemann
Columbia Theological Seminary
Palm Sunday 2020

1

REAPING THE WHIRLWIND

Leviticus, Exodus, Job

Our little systems have their day;
They have their day and cease to be;
They are but broken lights of thee,
And thou, O Lord, art more than they.

—Tennyson, "In Memoriam A.H.H."

I don't see it as an act of God;
I see it as something no one saw coming.

—Donald J. Trump, March 19, 2020

The lingering impact of the virus has summoned our best science to respond to human emergency. That lingering impact has also invited fresh theological consideration. In what follows I will explore some complex interpretive options in the Old Testament concerning the coming of the "plague" that in some way or another, in biblical horizon, is inflected by the reality of God. It is possible to trace out in the Old Testament at least three (maybe more!) interpretive options for such a God-linked reality of the plague.

THE TRANSACTIONAL MODE OF COVENANT

The first and most obvious interpretive possibility is *the transactional mode of covenant*. That transactional mode is based on the simple premise that in a tightly ordered world "good people prosper" and "evil people suffer." Covenant requires obedience to commandments. Obedience is rewarded; disobedience is punished. This calculus is readily articulated in Psalm 1:

> The LORD watches over the way of the righteous,
>> but the way of the wicked will perish. (Ps 1:6)

We can trace that reasoning in the two great recitals of blessing and curse in the Torah:

> If in spite of these punishments you have not turned back to me, but continue hostile to me, then I, too, will continue to be hostile to you. I myself will strike you sevenfold for your sins. I will bring the sword against you, executing vengeance for the covenant; and if you withdraw within your cities, I will send pestilence among you, and you shall be delivered into enemy hands. When I break your staff of bread, ten women shall bake your bread in a single oven, and they shall dole out your bread by weight; and though you eat, you shall not be satisfied. (Lev 26:23–26)

The phrasing is exactly symmetrical: you are hostile—I will be hostile! Divine hostility takes the form of a *sword* of vengeance; upon retreat from battle there comes *pestilence*; and the result of pestilence is *famine*. Thus we get the great triad of divine response. That triad, moreover, is readily seen in sequence. From war there may come pestilence and from pestilence there may come famine. This is the outcome, described in advance, for violation of Torah.

There is no uncertainty. These curses are not a natural threat. They are simply statement of the future Israel may choose by the way it orders its life.

We are able to see this same triad in play in the narrative of David (2 Sam 24:12–13) in the divine response to the royal census. It is noteworthy that David chooses pestilence in order to submit to direct divine action rather than suffer from the "human hands" of the sword. David trusts that even in this divine response, he may find "mercy" that he will not find in human interaction. In 2 Chr 20:9, moreover, prayer in the temple is offered as the one and only antidote to this triad of divine judgment. The same triad shows up as "the horsemen of the Apocalypse" (Rev 6:8). The matter is tightly transactional with no slippage: a pure quid pro quo.

The same reasoning is voiced in the second recital of curses, though with expansive exposition:

> The LORD will make the pestilence cling to you until it has consumed you off the land that you are entering to possess. The LORD will afflict you with consumption, fever, inflammation, with fiery heat, and drought, and with blight and mildew . . . The LORD will cause you to be defeated before your enemies . . . A people whom you do not know will eat up the fruit of your ground and of all your labors; you shall be continually abused and crushed, and driven mad by the sight that your eyes shall see. (Deut 28:21–34)

The cause of such trouble is that "You have forsaken me" (v. 20). After pestilence in v. 21, the sword is signaled in v. 25, and in vv. 30–33 there will be famine because of the seizure of all food by the enemy. This is the same as Leviticus 26; again, there is no slippage in the transaction.

In a general way, the prophetic "lawsuits" share the premise of *obedience/disobedience* and *blessing/curse*. In prophetic rhetoric, covenantal *commandment* issues in *indictment* for disobedience and *curse* becomes *prophetic judgment*. The logic is the same. That logic is pervasive in prophetic discourse. It is most intense and acute in Jeremiah and Ezekiel, likely because these particular traditions are closest to the final demise of contrary Judah. Thus Jeremiah's concern for false prophets, surely informed and shaped by the tradition of Deuteronomy:

> Here are the prophets saying to them,
> "You shall not see the sword,
>   nor shall you have famine,
>   but I will give you true peace in this place."
> (Jer 14:13)

In 15:2, Jeremiah reiterates the triad and adds a fourth element, captivity; but the pattern is the same:

> Those destined for pestilence, to *pestilence,*
>   and those destined for the sword, to the *sword;*
> those destined for famine, to *famine,*
>   and those destined for captivity, to *captivity.*

The prophetic tradition regularly and frequently reiterates the triad of coming trouble for the city (Jer 21:9; 24:10; 29:18; 32:36; 34:17; 38:2; 42:17, 22; 44:13; it will be noted that most of these uses are in prose that no doubt reflect subsequent editing). It is clear that in this important covenantal trajectory of interpretation, the transactional assumptions of covenant are in full play. The same reiteration is evident in the nearest contemporary of Jeremiah, namely, Ezekiel (Ezek 6:11; 7:15; 12:16).

This quid pro quo calculus in the Deuteronomy-covenantal tradition employed by the prophets becomes the ground for the judgment that Jerusalem was destroyed by YHWH for covenantal violation. Thus "the plague" (along with sword and famine) is an instrument of divine punishment against those who violate the covenantal order of creation willed by God.

Such reasoning may indeed strike us as brutalizing and repulsive given what we would regard as more "reasonable" interpretive categories. We may, however, linger over this reasoning for two reasons. First, this calculus is grounded in the conviction that God's creation is ordered according to a reliable moral intention that is non-negotiable. This most elemental conviction about reliability is not, in my judgment, to be dismissed lightly because such

4

reliability does not yield to relativity or situational nuance. It leaves for us a chance for wonderment: Is there indeed a line in the sand? A second reason for attending to this calculus is that it is the uncritical assumption of many very well-intended, serious people. It is that same "base line" into which we inculcate our children from early on. We do believe and trust that there are non-negotiable givens of moral coherence in the world even though their exact content is not clear or readily agreed upon. Indeed, it is the critical work of science to continue to probe such matters.

YHWH'S PURPOSEFUL ENACTMENT OF FORCE

A second interpretive trajectory exhibits YHWH's *purposeful enactment of force* in order to implement the *specific purpose of YHWH*. This trajectory is different from that of the transactive mode traced above because there is in this exhibit of force no explicit quid pro quo. A quid pro quo may sometimes be tacit and inferred, but it is not expressed. The accent is on the purposeful resolve of YHWH's force.

The normative exhibit of this trajectory, of course, is the sequence of "plagues" (smitings) in the Exodus narrative. This sequence of ten episodes features destructive actions against Pharaoh's Egypt in order that the slave community of Hebrews may be liberated from the brutality of Pharaoh. That sequence of ten episodes constitutes ten mighty exhibits of power in order that Pharaoh may discern the power and wonder of YHWH. It is proper to term these dramatic narrative encounters "miracles" as long as the term is understood as an exhibit of holy, divine power (not as "a violation of natural order"). Attempts have been made to "explain" the sequence of plagues as a chain of natural cause-and-effect events whereby one natural event triggers the next. That, however, is to miss the point of the narrative. The aim is to exhibit the capacity of the creator God to mobilize the various elements of creation in the service of divine intentionality.

That divine intentionality in the Exodus narrative is precisely that the community of Hebrew slaves may be emancipated:

> I will free you from the burdens of the Egyptians and
> deliver you from slavery to them. I will redeem you with
> an outstretched arm and with mighty acts of judgment.
> (Exod 6:6)

The outcome of the deliverance is the making of a covenant bond
with the emancipated community:

> I will take you as my people, and I will be your God. You
> shall know that I am the LORD your God, who has freed
> you from the burdens of the Egyptians. (Exod 6:7)

The concluding formula of Exod 14:30 echoes the same
intentionality.

Alternatively, the Priestly tradition sees the Exodus as a
means whereby YHWH's honor is enhanced:

> I will harden Pharaoh's heart, and he will pursue them, so
> that I will gain glory for myself over Pharaoh and all his
> army; and the Egyptians shall know that I am the LORD.
> (Exod 14:4, 17)

Taken together, these two accents assert that YHWH's honor *en-hancement* is accomplished by acts of *emancipation* that require
purposeful action against Pharaoh. The two aims cannot be sepa-
rated. On the one hand, this exhibit of YHWH's force is in order
that Israel may know that YHWH is God (Exod 6:7; 7:17; 10:2;
11:7). On the other hand, it is in order that Egypt may know that
YHWH is God (Exod 7:5; 8:10, 22; 9:29–30; 14:18). *Israel and
Egypt* together are instructed through this exhibit of divine power
that takes violent form.

*The purposefulness of YHWH's mobilization of destructive
power* set loose in Pharaoh's domain, moreover, is honed with
precision. This is evident in the affirmation that YHWH makes
a distinction between Egypt and Israel so that the utilization of
destructive power has a specific identifiable historical target:

> But the LORD will make a distinction between the live-
> stock of Israel and the livestock of Egypt, so that nothing
> shall die of all that belongs to the Israelites. (Exod 9:4)

And the LORD rained hail on the land of Egypt; there was hail with fire flashing continually in the midst of it, such heavy hail as had never fallen in all the land of Egypt since it became a nation. The hail struck down everything that was in the open field throughout all the land of Egypt, both human and animal; the hail also struck down all the plants of the field, and shattered every tree in the field. Only in the land of Goshen, where the Israelites were, there was no hail. (Exod 9:23–26)

Every firstborn in the land of Egypt shall die, from the firstborn of Pharaoh who sits on his throne to the first born of the female slave who is behind the handmill, and all the firstborn of the livestock. Then there will be a loud cry throughout all the land of Egypt, such as has never been or will ever be again. But not a dog shall growl at any of the Israelites—not at people, not at animals—so that you may know that the LORD makes a distinction between Egypt and Israel. (Exod 11:5–7)

The narrative is at pains to assert that this wild destructive "force of nature" is not random or indifferent to historical distinction. This claim of intention in the exhibit of force goes with the awareness that the destructive action is not any "natural event"; it is the accomplishment of an intentional agent who has a specific historical intent. This historical intentionality is further elucidated in the doxological rendition of the plagues in Ps 105:26–36. The destruction is portrayed as wholesale in Egypt. The adversative conjunction of v. 37 marks the contrast between devastated Egypt and emancipated Israel:

> *Then* he brought Israel out with silver and gold,
>> and there was no one among their tribes who stumbled.
> (Ps 105:37)

Amid the devastation, Israel is unscathed! It is impossible to read the Exodus narrative without recognition that the destructive plagues are purposeful, propelled by intentional agency and aimed at a particular historical circumstance, namely, the emergence of a new historical people Israel (see Exod 4:22).

A second such show of destructive force is articulated in the remarkable poem of Isa 2:12–17, a poem that is dominated by the word "against" that YHWH executes. These verses are framed in vv. 10 and 19 by a warning to flee into hiding before the terror of YHWH. That warning, moreover, is laden with the further awareness that there will be nowhere to hide from the divine terror.

> Enter into the rock,
>   and hide in the dust
> from the terror of the LORD,
>   and from the glory of his majesty.
>
> . . .
>
> For the LORD of hosts has a day
>   against all that is proud and lofty,
>   against all that is lifted up and high;
> against all the cedars of Lebanon,
>   lofty and lifted up;
>   and against all the oaks of Bashan;
> against all the high mountains,
>   and against all the lofty hills;
> against every high tower,
>   and against every fortified wall;
> against all the ships of Tarshish,
>   and against all the beautiful craft.
> The haughtiness of people shall be humbled,
>   and the pride of everyone shall be brought low;
>   and the LORD alone will be exalted on that day.
>
> . . .
>
> Enter the caves of the rocks
>   and the holes of the ground,
> from the terror of the LORD,
>   and from the glory of his majesty,
>   when he rises to terrify the earth.

The target of the terror of YHWH is identified only by poetic allusion: proud, lofty, lifted up, high, cedars of Lebanon, oaks of Bashan, high mountains, lofty hills, high tower, fortified wall, ships of Tarshish, beautiful craft, haughtiness. The imagery tumbles out! None of it is precise until we refer to the context of Isaiah. Then we can notice that the allusions are to commercial and military matters. In context, of course, the poetry refers to the royal-temple establishment in Jerusalem that the prophet takes as a visible, historical, political enactment of God-defying hubris. The mode of assault and attack against that establishment is left unnamed. The imagery could suggest a mighty wind—a force of nature—that will blow down the great trees. In context, however, it is likely that the threat is the mobilization of Assyria (and later the threat of Babylon).

The prophet is here not concerned with secondary causes. It is not "the day of the wind" or of Assyria or of Babylon. It is "the day of YHWH"! YHWH will mobilize the force that will terrorize the commercial-military establishment the prophet has in purview. Chapter 2 ends with an imperative to turn away from "The Man" (v. 22). "The Man" has only breath that is the gift of the creator and merits no regard. "The Man" in context surely refers to the "royal man" who presides in Jerusalem but who turns out to be quite penultimate. He is incapable of withstanding the mighty force of the creator God, who decisively impinges upon the security system of "The Man."

These verses themselves suggest no quid pro quo that would evoke the devastation. It is enough to see that the terror of YHWH is mobilized in order to preserve and enhance the rule of YHWH against usurpatious pride. It is evident that earlier verses in the chapter provide ground for a quid pro quo as Jerusalem is:

— Full of diviners and soothsayers

— Full of silver and gold

— Full of horses and chariots

— Full of idols (vv. 6–8)

The religious brokers will not save. The royal treasury will not save. The military establishment will not save. The idols will not save; Israel will throw them away in order to travel lightly into the caves. The security system of "The Man" is impotent and irrelevant before the terror of YHWH!

These two texts taken together, from Exodus and Isaiah, bespeak the capacity and resolve of YHWH to act in massively destructive ways against any historical ordering that contradicts the intent of YHWH. YHWH, it turns out, has many tools of sovereignty beyond the force of love. We may refer to David's conviction in 2 Samuel 24 that even the "pestilence" of YHWH may have a dimension of mercy to it. That dimension, however, was not made available to Pharaoh or to the targets of the poem of Isaiah. Only belatedly, long after the Exodus memory, it is allowed that even Egypt may be heard and healed:

> The LORD will strike Egypt,
>   striking and healing;
> they will return to the LORD,
>   and he will listen to their supplication and heal them.
>   (Isa 19:22)

That, however, will happen only after much smiting and after an abrupt "turn to the Lord."

YHWH'S HOLINESS ENACTED IN FREEDOM

Beyond any *tight quid pro quo* and beyond *the purposeful mobilization of violent force in the service of sovereignty*, we may identify a third interpretive possibility concerning the destructive action of God. This third possibility concerns the sheer holiness of God that God can enact in utter freedom without reason, explanation, or accountability, seemingly beyond any purpose at all. The classic textual example is in the whirlwind speeches in the book of Job where God declares that God's forceful creative actions are beyond any capacity of Job to master, explain, or comprehend. God, moreover, intends that God's actions should expose Job's anemic capacity for understanding. One can cite almost any text from those speeches:

> Where were you when I laid the foundation of the earth?
>   Tell me, if you have understanding.
> Who determined its measurements—surely you know!
>   Or who stretched the line upon it?

On what were its bases sunk,
  or who laid its cornerstone
when the morning stars sang together
  and all the heavenly beings shouted for joy?
Or who shut in the sea with doors
  when it burst out from the womb?—
when I made the clouds its garment,
  and thick darkness its swaddling band,
and prescribed bounds for it,
  and set bars and doors,
and said, "Thus far shall you come, and no farther;
  and here shall your proud waves be stopped"?
  (Job 38:4–11; see 38:31–33; 39:1–2, 9–12; 41:1–7)

God addresses Job with questions. God probes Job to see how far Job is able to engage the wonder of God's performance. Thus, the questions posed by God to Job are acts of defiance and put down; Job cannot answer. God knows very well that God's own wondrous work is fully beyond the ken of Job. God appeals to Job's competence and then arrives at a triumphant "then," asserting that Job can never replicate the lordly action of God. Job will have no victory over the bottomless capacity of God!

Then I will also acknowledge to you
  that your own right hand can give you victory. (Job 40:14)

Job cannot answer because Job has no capacity for answering. YHWH's defiant questions have put Job in his proper place as a dependent creature with clear limitations that he is wont to deny. He cannot ever catch up to God's glorious sovereignty that is cast in holiness. In the rhetoric of dismissive questions, God is exhibited as "wholly other," as completely unlike Job and not at all subject to Job's mode of knowledge or categories of explanation. Job is brought to an awareness that he stands before a sovereignty he cannot penetrate:

See, I am of small account;
  what shall I answer you? (Job 40:4)

Job's final response is an acknowledgment of God's capacity for freedom that need not answer to Job's small insistent probes:

> I know that you can do all things,
> > and that no purpose of yours can be thwarted. (Job 42:2)

Job's final utterance in 42:6 is inescapably ambiguous. That ambiguity, however, can only follow Job's admission of his own limit.

It was Tod Linafelt who first suggested to me that *The Idea of the Holy* by Rudolf Otto is a useful reference point for reading the poetry of Job. It will be remembered from Otto that the *tremendum* of God's holiness is both *fascinating and threatening*. That is how God is presented in the book of Job. There is a compelling freshness about God who is offered with artistic style in Job. At the same time, however, there is a dangerousness that the God before whom Job must stand does not offer closeness, intimacy, or fidelity. This God has no obligation for such availability. Otto's "sublime" concerns greatness that is beyond calculation that evokes awe but at the same time off-putting distance. It is no wonder that the Priestly interpreters in ancient Israel and in the ancient world generally attempted to corral holiness into manageable, administratable categories (see, for example, Deut 14:1–21). The early narratives of 1 Sam 6:19–20 and 2 Sam 6:6–11 concerning the ark, however, attest an awareness that the holiness of God cannot be presumed upon. That dangerous holiness of God defies the domesticating efforts of the ancient priests even as it escapes the efforts of modern science.

The outcome of this trajectory concerning God's holiness is the recognition that God will not be entrapped in our best efforts. God may and will do wild things beyond our hopes or expectations. Thus, the "wonders" that God performs in creation and in history are beyond expectation or administration. Both Job and his friends sought to reduce God to their quid pro quo explanations. But the God who emerges in the whirlwind will do otherwise, and their reasoning is ineffective before God.

We can identify subsequent echoes of this strange outcome of the poem of Job. While the poem of Job remains in the sphere of creation, Israel's tradition boldly carries the same affirmation into the sphere of history. Thus, concerning God's demolition of Assyria, there is nothing Assyria can do against such divine resolve. The prophetic poem ends in this defiant declaration:

> For the LORD of hosts has planned, and who can annul it?
> His hand is stretched out, and who will turn it back?
> (Isa 14:27)

The answer is, "No one will annul; no one will turn it back!" No one can annul or turn it back because the holy one of Israel has declared that purpose. Such a claim renders penultimate all of our best management of the historical process. In like manner concerning YHWH's dealing with and through Babylon, the prophet dismisses those in Israel who question God's intent:

> Woe to you who strive with your Maker,
> earthen vessels with the potter!
> Does the clay say to the one who fashions it,
> "What are you making?"
> or "Your work has no handles"?
> Woe to anyone who says to a father, "What are you begetting?"
> or to a woman, "With what are you in labor?" (Isa 45:9–10)

Israel has no warrant to question YHWH; YHWH acts freely and need not give account. Belatedly, even Nebuchadnezzar learned the hard way:

> All the inhabitants of the earth are accounted as nothing,
> and he dozes what he wills with the host of heaven and the
> inhabitants of the earth.
> There is no one who can stay his hand
> or say to him, "What are you doing?" (Dan 4:35)

No one! No one can question. And even such an innocent looking text as the book of Proverbs allows, as Gerhard von Rad has seen, that in the end, God acts inscrutably, human intent notwithstanding:

> The human mind may devise many plans,
> but it is the purpose of the LORD that will be established.
> (Prov 19:21; see also 16:2, 9; 20:24; 21:2, 30–31)

YHWH does not offer explanation, as both Israel and Nebuchadnezzar learned. Life lived in God's world requires coming to terms with the inscrutability of God that defies all limitation and all efforts at domestication.

In light of this exposition we may recognize in biblical testimony three angles of vision for our interpretive work concerning the onslaught of a plague:

— A *transactional quid pro quo* that issues in punishment for violators;

— A *purposeful mobilization of negative force* in order to effect God's own intent, and

— A *raw holiness* that refuses and defies our best explanations, so that God's force is an irreducible reality in the world.

HIDDEN THINGS

None of these interpretive options is of much use or interest in the midst of the virus. We do not have energy or inclination for such matters when more closely we are preoccupied with germs, infections, contagion, pandemic, and a general sense of jeopardy. In a word, we want science that can be effectively administered through responsible political channels. We want experts who can be trusted and who will provide relief from both threat and anxiety. And we want political administrators who have the courage and honesty to make effective antidotes available to us without deception or denial.

That is what we want and must have, and nothing more. And, of course, biblical faith is not in any way inimical to such science that probes into what seems ahead of time as the inscrutability of creation. Sometimes the church has been fearful of science (Galileo!); that, however, is not the case for the Bible. (We can recognize that the Bible is indeed inimical to *scientism* of the kind fostered by some of the neo-atheists. Such scientism seeks to make the work of science into the master-narrative of worldly reality—a claim that it cannot sustain.)

But while being fully appreciative of responsible scientific work, the Bible at the same time is fully cognizant of the limitation of such work. In the singular poem of Job 28, the poem endorses human exploration of the earth and gladly affirms gains made by such probes:

> The sources of the rivers they [miners] probe;
> hidden things they bring to light. (vv. 11)

But then the poem reverses field to ask:

> But where shall wisdom be found?
> And where is the place of understanding? (vv. 12, 20)

And then comes answer:

> God understands the way to it,
> and he knows its place.
> For he looks to the end of the earth,
> and sees everything under the heavens.
> When he gave to the wind its weight,
> and apportioned out the waters by measure;
> when he made a decree for the rain,
> and a way for the thunderbolt;
> then he saw it, and declared it;
> he established it, and searched it out. (vv. 23–27)

God knows! And then the poet draws a conclusion concerning human engagement with the mystery of creation:

> Truly, the fear of the LORD, that is wisdom;
> and to depart from evil is understanding. (v. 28)

True knowledge is finally not in scientific exploration but in the fear of YHWH and the shunning of evil. Important as it surely is, scientific exploration has its limits.

More directly, a proverb makes a categoric distinction between the inscrutability of the creator God and the work of human investigation:

It is the glory of God to conceal things,
    but the glory of kings to search things out. (Prov 25:2)

Human investigation (characteristically funded by governments, often in the service of the military), seeks to "search things out." That is the proper work of human curiosity and, as with the virus, an urgent human need. The second line in the proverb, however, is matched by the first line concerning God's proper work. Thus, *human searching* out and *God's concealment* are the endless riddling process concerning the wonder of creation. There are limits to seeking things out, not in the form of prohibition but in the endless capacity of God to conceal. The claim of the proverb, however, is that divine concealment will always run beyond human searching out, so that science will always have more work to do but will not finally, according to the proverb, master the mystery of creation. The enterprise is an on-going cat and mouse game. The cat will prevail; but the game requires energetic and brave mice as well. Sometimes a wily mouse may outwit the cat for an instant! The human scientific enterprise is indeed to search things out; that enterprise does not and need not linger too much over the three trajectories of faith that I have exposited. And in the midst of a pandemic, we surely will not linger there.

MYSTERY THAT GOES DEEPER

So why bother with the interpretive categories of biblical faith when in fact our energy and interest are focused on more immediate matters? The answer is simple and obvious. We linger because, in the midst of our immediate preoccupation with our felt jeopardy and our hope for relief, our imagination does indeed range beyond the immediate to larger, deeper wonderments. Our free-ranging imagination is not finally or fully contained in the immediacy of our stress, anxiety, and jeopardy. Beyond these demanding immediacies, we have a deep sense that our life is not fully contained in the cause-and-effect reasoning of the Enlightenment that seeks to explain and control. There is *more than that* and *other than that* to our life in God's world!

I became acutely aware of that "more and other" when my friend Peter Block commented on the virus. Peter is a Jewish secular guy not prone to meta-commentary. Nonetheless he said, "The virus is God's way of ending consumerism; it is the end of the narrative of globalism." Peter's utterance was likely not a sober critical theological judgment. But he said it knowingly, and in his cunning way he meant exactly that. He meant, I take it, that the narrative of globalism and its conceit that we may master and use up the resources of the earth in our indifferent indulgence will fail. They will fail because such practices contradict the given reality of creation and the will of the creator. To speak of such limit does not make it necessary to render God as a character or an agent. But Peter did! And we do! We do so partly out of tradition, piety, and force of habit. But we also move to name God because we are confronted with mystery that goes deeper than our "searching out." It turns out that such God-talk does not situate God at the edge of our life or as "God of the gaps," but attests God in, with, and under the several processes of creation. This God who will not be mocked—not by Pharaoh or by Assyria or by Babylon or by any contemporary embodiment of hubris.

Tennyson does not insist that God causes our "little system" to cease, only that they cease to be. That is what my friend Peter noticed, that our "little system" is ceasing to be. It is a cessation caused by a will that exceeds our categories. It does not matter if we name such an assault as an "act of God" or, with Trump, name it otherwise. Both Tennyson and Trump recognize, in different idioms, that such an assault is undoubtedly beyond our management or explanation. The reason none saw it coming is because it has come from beyond our world of knowledge or control, from an elsewhere that is laden with inscrutability. We arrive, in our honesty and fear, at the unspeakable for which our faith tradition has provided proximate language.

Thus it is possible, when pressed beyond our explanation, to speak according to our faith tradition about the virus:

— It is possible to think about *a transactional quid pro quo*; we reap what we sow in a world governed by the creator God. Some practice and policies may evoke wrath. So Job and his friends!

— It is possible to think about *the purposeful mobilization of the negative forces of creation* to perform the intention of the creator God, plagues that defy every "high tower" and every "fortified wall."

— It is possible to pause before God's *raw holiness* in a world that is not tamed by our best knowledge.

None of this is possible in the world of modern Enlightenment rationality. The church, however, has long understood that that modernist narrative is not adequate for the mystery of creation. In times of emergency, it is possible (and necessary?) to step outside that modern narrative and to take a peek into the vast claim of creator and creation. It will be only a peek, not a permanent habitation. But the peek might be revelatory and transformative.

The preacher has amazing interpretive resources available for such a season of wonderment. The wonderment does come, perhaps at night, perhaps in the midst of quarantine. It comes upon us because we are gifted with imagination that will not settle for explanation. We are often, soon or late, pressed to ask about "the fear of the LORD" and "the shunning of evil." In our imagined autonomy we have, in the global narrative, been on a spree of self-indulgence and self-actualization that has exercised little regard for the neighbor. And now we are required to wonder more deeply. It is the work of the preacher to authorize and guide such wonderment. The *end* of such wonder may happily come in the form of a vaccine. But its *beginning* is in the fear of the Lord. This is a lesson learned always too late, too late for Pharaoh, too late for Nebuchadnezzar . . . always too late . . . or just in time!

Finally this, dear preachers: We preachers are not mandated to live within the confines of modern rationality. We are, rather, called to bear witness to another realm, the vast governance (kingdom!) of God that encompasses our modernist logic. That vast governance, on our lips, may outflank the fearful logic of the Enlightenment, will surely judge it, and may in mercy redeem it.

Peeking into Mystery

Creator God, you have entrusted to us knowledge of good and evil.
    You have permitted us knowledge of the world in which we live,
    and
    that knowledge has yielded immense gains for us,
    gains of control, of productivity, of explanation, of connections
    of causes and effects.
Only rarely—like now!—do we collide with
    your hiddenness that summons us and embarrasses us.
    We peek into your awesome hidden presence;
    we find our certitudes quite disrupted.
Thus we pause at the edge of your holiness,
        finding that your unfathomable presence is an odd mix
        of mercy and judgment,
        of generosity and accountability,
        of forgiveness and starchy realism.
We dwell at the edge of your mystery for an instant . . . not longer.
    Then we return to our proper work of knowledge, research,
    explanation, and management.
By that instant, however, we are changed . . . sobered, summoned,
emancipated, filled with wonder
    before your holiness.
It is for that holiness that outflanks us that we give you thanks.
Amen.

2

PESTILENCE . . . MERCY?
WHO KNEW?

2 Samuel 24:1–25

As an Old Testament teacher, it is not a big stretch for me to try to segue from the current virus to Old Testament talk about "pestilence" and "plague." Of course, I understand that they are not exact equivalents, but they are close enough to invite imagination and reflection. In making that segue I have been astonished to find this odd narrative in 2 Sam 24:1–25 that ends in "pestilence." I term the narrative "odd" because in a "primitive" way God is voiced as a real character and an engaged agent who speaks and acts. That, of course, is enough for us to readily disregard the text. I suggest nonetheless it is worth lingering over the story.

The premise of the narrative is that the King David has been "incited" by God in a royal act. (In the parallel text of 1 Chr 21:1–13 it is "Satan" who incites.) Either way, David is seduced into conducting a census; a census is of course a tool of the state (see Luke 2:1) that is most often designed in order to administer: (a) the tax rolls or (b) the manpower roster for military conscription. Subsequently, David is aware that such a royal act in "numbering the people" is a sin in which he has acted "very foolishly." He must answer for his foolishness, because God in whom he trusts is not big on either tax rolls or military rosters (2 Sam 24:10).

PESTILENCE AND CURSE

Background to this narrative is the classic Near Eastern triad of curses: "sword, famine, *pestilence.*" That triad is voiced in the classic Israelite recitals of curse:

> I will bring the *sword* against you . . .
> I will send *pestilence* against you . . .
> I *break your staff of bread.*
> (Lev 26:25–26; see Deut 28:21–34)

It is, moreover, a triad repeated in prophetic oracles of judgment that implement the covenant curses of YHWH, most especially in the traditions of Jeremiah and Ezekiel:

> Those destined for pestilence, to *pestilence,*
> and those destined for the sword, to *the sword;*
> those destined for famine, to *famine,*
> and those destined for captivity, to *captivity.* (Jer 15:2)[1]

> For they shall fall by the *sword,* by *famine,* and by
> *pestilence.* (Ezek 6:11)[2]

While the triad recurs almost by rote reiteration, it does refer to real-life troubles that may beset a society. Even such rote reiteration grows from and is informed by real-life experience.

THREE OPTIONS FOR PUNISHMENT

In response to David's readiness to atone for his foolish sin, YHWH answers, most remarkably, by offering David three options of punishment according to the three classic curses. The narrative exhibits no wonderment about YHWH's direct response to David, nor concerning YHWH's imposing on David responsibility

---

1. See further, Jer 21:9; 24:10; 29:18; 32:36; 34:17; 38:2; 42:17; 44:13.
2. See further, Ezek 7:15; 12:16.

for "choosing his own poison." David must choose from three not very good alternatives. He may opt for:

three years of *famine*, or
three months of *sword*, or
three days of *pestilence*.

The pattern of three/three/three (three curses in three different time frames) is a pattern familiar from folk narrative. Thus, David not only faces a terrible punishment but also must take responsibility for selecting it.

David's response to YHWH is terse and prompt. He chooses the three days of pestilence as a way to "take away guilt." We are not told that David makes his choice because the time of suffering is shorter. Rather, he makes the choice because pestilence comes directly from YHWH. He prefers direct action from YHWH rather than famine, which will no doubt feature the effect of human advantage for some at the expense of others, not unlike cutbacks on SNAP provisions for poor people. He chooses direct action from YHWH rather than war, for he knows from experience how brutal human war can be. (See David's own brutality in war in 1 Sam 18:25–27.) By contrast—note well!—David anticipates that in the midst of pestilence from YHWH he may receive mercy. He will take his chances on YHWH rather than to fall into human hands! YHWH's mercy is great (24:14)!

In context, this is an incredible mouthful! David knows he merits punishment. He does not seek to bargain or escape that future from YHWH. In the midst of his transactional realism, however, he remembers that his life, his position, and his power are grounded in the inexplicable mercy of YHWH. He relies on the free agency of YHWH who is not domesticated into transactional modes of relationship. YHWH may indeed disrupt the three days of pestilence with mercy; that is his best hope! The God who prescribes punishment is all the while the God of mercy who may mitigate the sentence.

HOPE ROOTED IN STEADFAST LOVE

We may notice that David's hope for YHWH's mercy is deeply rooted in his faith and in his narrative. In the most elemental promise made to David, YHWH avers:

> I will never take my steadfast love from him. (2 Sam 7:15)

(The term "steadfast love" is not the one in our verse, but both terms bespeak YHWH's covenantal solidarity.) The term in 2 Sam 7:15 (*hesed*) is reiterated as the final affirmation in David's long thanksgiving:

> He is a tower of salvation for his king,
>   and shows steadfast love to his anointed,
>   to David and his descendants forever. (2 Sam 22:51)

While the term "steadfast love" (*hesed*) recurs in the narrative, in our verse David appeals to the more radical term "mercy" (*rhm*), which is cognitively linked to the term for "womb" (*rhm*), suggesting an intimate embracive connection, as in the wordplay of Isa 49:15:

> Can a woman forget her nursing child,
>   or show no compassion (*rhm*) for the child of her womb (*rhm*)?

David appeals to YHWH's most elemental granular commitment to David. Even this dread moment does not detract David from that hope and conviction. David knew, according to the psalm, that,

> He will not always accuse,
>   nor will he keep his anger forever.
> He does not deal with us according to our sins,
>   nor repay us according to our iniquities. (Ps 103:9–10)

He counted on the affirmation of the psalm:

> For he will deliver you from snare of the fowler
>   and from the deadly *pestilence* . . .

You will not fear the terror of the night,
    or the arrow that flies by day
or the *pestilence* that stalks in darkness,
    or the destruction that wastes at noonday. (Ps 91:3–6)

So YHWH's punishment is enacted, and the death-toll was great:

> So the LORD sent a pestilence on Israel from that morn-
> ing until the appointed time; and seventy thousand of
> the people died, from Dan to Beer-sheba. But when the
> angel stretched out his hand toward Jerusalem to destroy
> it, the LORD relented concerning the evil, and said to the
> angel who was bringing destruction among the people,
> "It is enough; now stay your hand." The angel of the
> LORD was then by the threshing floor of Araunah the
> Jebusite. When David saw the angel who was destroying
> the people, he said to the LORD: "I alone have sinned,
> and I alone have done wickedly; but these sheep, what
> have they done? Let your hand, I pray, be against me and
> against my father's house." (2 Sam 24:15–17)

The conclusion includes David buying Araunah's threshing floor
in order to build an altar, the offering of sacrifices, and YHWH
answering his prayer of supplication (vv. 24–25). The story conse-
quently conveys YHWH acting in judgment as well as answering
prayer and extending mercy.

AN INVITATION TO OPEN IMAGINATION

I do not think for one moment that there is any ready transfer
from this narrative to our real-life crisis with the virus. The Bible
does not often easily "apply." The Bible does, however, invite an
open imagination that hopes for the best outcomes of serious
scientific research. At the same time, it affirms that deeply inscru-
table holy reality is in, with, under, and beyond our best science.
Thus, in the calculus of David's transactional world, he knows that
foolish decisions and actions may evoke unwelcome outcomes.
He knows, at the same time, that a hovering holiness could rule
otherwise. So now we witness a virus that may possibly be linked

to our ambitious ordering of reality. We meet, pray, sing, and hope in our exercise of faith, nonetheless, that beyond every quid pro quo there is more and other.

It is most impossible to see the virus as something like a divine blowback to the hubris that has propelled the global narrative, its indulgent use of earth's resources, and its exploitation of the vulnerable. I note on the day that I write this that China has experienced an "unintentional consequence" of the virus, namely, a clear sky without the smog of over-loaded street traffic. Who knew? The virus may indeed amount to a curbing of our worst social habits and invite a slow-down to the pace of creation's reality. It may lead to gentler treatment of prisoners and a more generous offer to the left behind. We may dare imagine with David that the final word is not pestilence; it is mercy.

On Counting and Being Accountable

As required by our Constitution we are amid a census;
   our government wants to know how, and how many,
      wants to have all the data it can mobilize.
We have been counting forever:
   Caesar counted and sent folk to Bethlehem to sign up;
      before Caesar, no doubt Pharaoh and Tiglath-Pileser and
      Nebuchadnezzar counted;
         after Caesar, Constantine, the Holy Roman Empire,
         and every modern nation state counted . . . all counted!
All count! To have a complete roster for the military draft;
   to have a list for the IRS.
Our father in faith, David, counted.
And then! He had to answer;
   he had to pay for his pride;
   he had to be brought back to his proper penultimate place.
When he chose his poison, he chose you!
He chose you as his judge, over the threat of natural disaster,
      over the prospect of human brutality.
He chose you, because he reckoned you, in your judgment, filled
with mercy.
We in our prideful counting are answerable to you;
   facing the cost of our pride, we choose you;
   We choose you and your compassion;
   We choose you; because we trust that,
      you do not deal with us according to our sins,
      nor repay us according to our iniquities.
So we choose you . . . and begin again, chastened and filled with
fresh possibility. Amen.

3

UNTIL THE DANCING
BEGINS AGAIN

Jeremiah

I have been noticing (as we all have) that graduations are being
cancelled and weddings are being postponed. Amid the virus is
no time for assemblages of joyous celebration. In the time of the
disaster of ancient Jerusalem, Jeremiah noticed the same thing.
Three times he observes that weddings are cancelled in Jerusalem
because it is no time to celebrate and no time to bet on the future.

— In 7:34, Jeremiah notices the end of weddings as the
corpses pile up:

> The corpses of his people will be food for the birds of the
> air, and for the animals of the earth . . . And I will bring to
> an end the sound of mirth and gladness, the voice of the
> bride and bridegroom in the cities of Judah and in the
> streets of Jerusalem; for the land shall become a waste.

— In 16:9, Jeremiah notices that they are not even having
funerals, let alone wedding feasts:

> Both great and small shall die . . . and no one shall lament
> of them; you shall not go into the house of feasting to

> sit with them, to eat and drink . . . I am going to banish
> from this place, in your days and before your eyes the
> voice of mirth and the voice do gladness, the voice of the
> bridegroom and the voice of the bride.

— In 25:10 Jeremiah anticipates that the land will become a ruin and a waste:

> And will banish from them the sound of mirth and the
> sound of gladness, the voice of the bridegroom and the
> voice of the bride . . . This whole land shall become a ruin
> and a waste.

More than any other witness in the Old Testament, Jeremiah leans most deeply and most honestly into the disaster of his people. He takes the failure of social assemblies as a sign of the death of the city. When the city cannot assemble for rites of passage, it is sure evidence that social life has failed. Indeed, among us, it is only the foolish who insist on assembling, among them pastors who insist that Jesus will protect us from the virus. My pastor rightly calls such folk "knuckleheads." Jeremiah could not even identify any such knuckleheads because the whole world of social possibility had been shut down.

Three times Jeremiah uses the odd term *htn* that is rendered "bridegroom" only here in our texts and in Joel 2:16. (See its metaphorical use in the familiar texts of Ps 19:5; Isa 61:10; 62:5.) But then, belatedly, the prophet in his promissory utterance uses the term a fourth time in anticipation. This time, he is able to envision a resumption of weddings as young people and their families are willing once again to bet on and invest in the future:

> There shall once more be heard the voice of mirth and
> the voice of gladness, the voice of the bridegroom and
> the voice of the bride, the voices of those who sing, as
> they bring thank offerings to the house of the LORD.
> (Jer 33:10–11)

The prophet anticipates that in this place of waste, disaster, and devastation the sounds of festival celebration will again be heard. Life will resume in its rich social thickness. Amid the sounds of social gladness there will be songs of thank offering sung to the God who restores and revivifies:

> Give thanks to the LORD of hosts,
> for the LORD is good,
> for his steadfast love endures forever! (Jer 33:11)

This is Israel's most elemental doxology. (See the repeated doxological formula in Ps 136.) At its best, Israel sings of YHWH's *ḥesed*, "steadfast love" that I have translated as "tenacious solidarity." This singing is the affirmation that God has not for an instant abandoned God's people or God's world but has been abidingly faithful, even through the devastation. Thus the *doxology* of v. 11 follows the *restoration of weddings* in v. 10. And then v. 11 ends with the reiteration of Jeremiah's' favorite phrase of restoration, "Restore the fortunes" (see Jer 29:14; 30:3, 18; 31:23; 32:44; 33:7, 27). This is the conventional translation of the oft-repeated phrase in Jeremiah. That translation, however, is inadequate because the prophetic promise does not intend a return to "the good old days" or a restoration of a previous political-economic arrangement under an oppressive royal regime. The phrase rather intends a return to the land of promise that will be ordered, organized, and lived out in freshly faithful ways. Thus it is "restoration" to the arena of God's promise, but not to a status that might invite some to nostalgia. God's "restoration" is characteristically toward a new historical possibility through the giving of new gifts. This God has the capacity to restore, recover, and revivify! This is *the God of homecoming* after there was displacement. This is *the God of Easter* who has not quit, not even on that dread Friday or that misery-lasting Saturday. It is no wonder that the older son in the parable heard "singing and dancing" (Luke 15:25). The reason for the singing and dancing is:

> This brother of yours was dead and has come to life;
> he was lost and has been found. (Luke 15:32)

The restoration can only be rendered in song and parable, two of the great trusts of the church! God's "restoration" is, perforce, rendered in song and parable because it is a newness that accommodates none of the categories or explanations known in the past.

This song of thanks that Jeremiah anticipates puts me in mind of the great German anthem of thanks, "Now Thank We All Our God." This best loved hymn of German Evangelicals was written by Pastor Martin Rinkart during the Thirty Years War (1618–1648) as a table grace for his family. The notice I have on this work by Pastor Rinkart offers this startling awareness:

> Martin Rinkart was pastor in Eilenburg, Saxony, the town of his birth. The walled city was a refuge for many fleeing war and pestilence. Left as the only clergyman in town, he often buried as many as forty or fifty persons in one day. Although his wife died of the pestilence, Rinkart survived.[1]

He wrote not only during the long-running war but in the face of pestilence that decimated the population as he presided over their many deaths. We do well to ponder this simple table prayer of gratitude amid pestilence:

> Now thank we all our God with hearts and hands and voices,
>   who wondrous things hath done, in whom this world rejoices;
> who, from our mothers' arms, hath blessed us on our way
>   with countless gifts of love, and still is ours today.
> O may this bounteous God through all our life be near us,
>   with ever joyful hearts and blessed peace to cheer us;
> and keep us in God's grace, and guide us when perplexed,
>   and free us from all ills in this world and the next.

The context of his work, not unlike our own, was a scene of relentless death. Yet Rinkart wrote and sang of thanks! The hymn celebrates the "wondrous things" done by "this bounteous God." We can picture Pastor Rinkart with his children counting out, one by one, "countless gifts of love." The hymn invites us to cling to God's grace that "frees us of all ills" in all imaginable futures. The

1. Forman, *New Century Hymnal Companion*, 421.

words are as sure, bold, and awe-filled as is Israel's best doxology in Jer 33:11.

The rhetoric of Jeremiah, echoed by this German prayer-hymn, provides clues for our ministry now. We may identify two accent points that recur in this rhetoric. First is to engage in *relentless, uncompromising hope*. This is more than a civic assurance that "we will get through this." It is rather the conviction that God will not quit until God has arrived at God's good intention. There is a purpose at work in, with, under, and beyond our best resolves. That holy purpose is tenacious, steadfast, and relentless, that we and all of God's creation will come to wellbeing. The task of the church is to hope in a way that is grounded in the good faithful resolve of God.

But the second task of ministry is the work in the meantime to be *witnesses to the abiding ḥesed (tenacious solidarity) of God* that persists amid pestilence. It is the witness of Jeremiah that in the midst of abandonment, God has not abandoned. Or to change the figure with Jeremiah, the seemingly barren wilderness is grace-occupied (Jer 31:2). That witness is performed by both word (at which we are pretty good!) and by act. The act is performed by neighborly gesture in a time of fear, by neighborly generosity and hospitality in a time of self-preoccupation, and by neighborly policies in the face of predatory greed. Who would have thought medical co-payments could be cancelled? Who would have anticipated the release of prisoners on their own reconnaissance? Who would have imagined that student debts and interest on those debts could be deferred? The work of the church is to empower and summon to such policies and to celebrate them as they appear among us. These new policies need not be aberrations for the sake of an emergency. They may indeed be the "new normal"!

The work of ministry is to render the virus as penultimate, to see that even its lethal force is outflanked by the goodness of God. Thus we have this simple witness of Pastor Rinkart with his willingness to sing and pray, even with death as close as his own household. Faith is indeed "the assurance of things hoped for, the conviction of things not seen" (Heb 11:1). That faith does not yield to death because it knows in the deepest ways that the goodness of God will not fold in the face of the threat of death. It boggles to know that that faith is entrusted to fallible folk like us. Jeremiah anticipated that the wedding, singing, and dancing would begin again, perhaps soon. In the meantime, he waited with truth-telling honesty and courage.

Let the Dance Begin . . . Soon

We now miss out on so much
    the graduation of a granddaughter,
    the wedding of a niece,
    the Final Four,
    the beginning of Baseball,
    the great Easter liturgy,
    the day by day interaction on the street.
The virus has imposed a huge silence among us.
It is a silence that evokes loneliness,
    and domestic violence,
    and job loss,
    and the end of life in the bars, and on the beach, and in the
    street.
We wait; we may wait in despair, or at least in deep disappointment.
But we may also wait differently:
    we wait in confident faith;
    we wait in eager longing.
    we wait on the Lord.
We wait for the future and against despair,
    because we know that you, the God of life, will defeat the force
    of death.
    We know that the Friday execution could not defeat the life lived
    by Jesus
        nor the life lived by his faithful people.
As we wait, we practice our next moves for the coming dance;
    it is only a little while . . . "yet a little while";
    we will *walk* the long march of obedience;
    we will *run* the race of discipleship;
    we will *soar* like eagles into God's good future of neighborliness.
We know that you will overcome the silence
    because the silence . . . no more than the darkness. . .
        can overcome the Lord of Life. Amen.

4

PRAYING AMID THE VIRUS

1 Kings 8:23–53

Be not dismayed what e're betide,
God will take care of you.[1]

It is essential that we should speak of prayer in detail because
in the first instance . . . prayer, or praying is simply asking.
—Karl Barth[2]

Let us approach the subject from the given fact that God
answers. He is not deaf, he listens; more than that, he acts.
He does not act in the same way whether we pray or not.
Prayer exerts an influence upon God's action, even upon his
existence. This is what the word "answer" means.
—Karl Barth[3]

It will disappear one day . . . like a miracle.

—Donald J. Trump

1. *United Methodist Hymnal*, 130.
2. Barth, *Church Dogmatics*, 3/3:268.
3. Barth, *Prayer according to the Catechisms of the Reformation*, 21.

W omen and men of faith, at our best, "pray without ceasing" (1 Thess 5:17). More than that, we pray passionately in times of need and crisis. We send our friends "thoughts and prayers" in times of their crises. In our current bewilderment and relative impotence in the face of the virus, we surely pray now for rescue and wellbeing for ourselves and for our world. Having thought about the interface of *virus* and *prayer*, I decided to look into that same interface in the Old Testament between *pestilence* and *prayer.*

PRAYER AND PESTILENCE
IN THE OLD TESTAMENT

One of the great prayers of the Old Testament is the prayer placed in the mouth of Solomon at the dedication of the Jerusalem temple (1 Kgs 8:23–53). The prayer of the king voices primary accents of the faith of Israel and is in part didactic according to the Deuteronomic tradition that shapes the narrative. In the center of the prayer is a long series of instances of disaster that will invite and evoke Israel's prayers to YHWH (vv. 31–53). This section of the prayer is introduced by a general petition asking that God should *hear, heed, and forgive* (v. 30). Then follow a series of seven cases of urgent need:

— sin against a neighbor (v. 31)

— defeat in war (v. 33)

— drought (v. 35)

— plague (pestilence!), blight, mildew (v. 37)

— prayer of a foreigner (v. 41)

— in time of war (v. 44)

— in captivity (v. 46)

In each case, the disaster is described. Each such disaster is followed by a petition, "Then hear" (vv. 32, 34, 35, 39, 43, 45, 49). That singular, insistent petitionary imperative is variously followed by a bid that God should act to "forgive" or to "maintain their cause." The sequence of petitions is based on the assumption that God can be mobilized to act in response to a lived emergency; God surely has the power and capacity to overcome the stated disaster when God is mobilized. The sequence of petitions concludes with a summary petition,

> Let your eyes be open to the plea of your servant, and to the plea of your people Israel, listening to them whenever they call to you. (v. 52)

Israel is ready to trust that God will listen and engage. That summary petition, moreover, reinforced by the final v. 53, which affirms God's singular commitment to Israel based on promises made to Moses:

> For you have separated them from among all the peoples of the earth, to be your heritage, as you promised through Moses, your servant, when you brought our ancestors out of Egypt, O Lord GOD. (v. 53)

This appeal is based on affirmations like the opening statement at Sinai in Exod 19:4-6.

This remarkable prayer insists and asserts that the temple now being dedicated is primarily an arena for prayers to YHWH; the main purpose of the temple is praying and being heard. It is affirmed that prayer is the effective antidote for every form of disaster. We may notice, however, that this statement of effective antidote is in form of trust and not a flat certitude. It is a genuine petition that trusts but does not know that YHWH will answer. That is, this is an interaction between two free agents and not a mechanical or automatic transaction.

The conclusion of 1 Kgs 8 reports the liturgy of dedication that culminates as a bid to worshiping Israel to be faithful to covenant:

> Incline our hearts to him, to walk in all his ways, and to keep his commandments, his statutes, and his ordinances, which he commanded our ancestors . . . Therefore devote yourselves completely to the LORD our God,

walking in his statutes and keeping his commandments,
as at this day. (vv. 58, 61)

That is, the extended set of petitions is situated in a context of covenantal attentiveness. The assumption of the prayer is an active,
trusting relationship that provides a context of hope in the midst
of every disaster. The reference to "pestilence" (plague) in v. 37
is only one of many named disasters. We may see in that verse,
however, that a trusting insistent prayer of petition is the proper
response of faith in the context of willing obedience. The govern-
ing imperative, "Then hear," is refined by "forgive and act . . ."
(v. 39). In the theology of the Deuteronomic tradition, forgiveness
becomes the precondition for moving forward to wellbeing. Effective covenantal fidelity becomes the basis and context for urgent
petition. It is, moreover, to be noted, concerning every specific
petition, there is no assurance that the petition "works." There is
only an insistence that it should be voiced in trust.

THE CHRONICLER'S SHIFTS

This prayer in 1 Kgs 8 is definitively important for the theology
that governs the narrative of 1 and 2 Kings and that makes the
temple the epicenter of Israel's life of faith. It is also indicates why
the subsequent destruction of the temple was such a grievous crisis
for Israel. The centrality of the temple for the life of faith is further
enhanced in this later parallel account of monarchic Israel in 1 and
2 Chronicles. The prayer of Solomon in 1 Kgs 8 is closely reiterated
in the presentation of the Chronicler in 2 Chr 6:14–42. In that version our accent on the plague (pestilence) occurs in vv. 28–31 with
reiteration of the same words. Only the conclusion of the prayer of
Solomon offers a significant variation in the Chronicler. In 1 Kgs 8,
as we have seen, the prayer concludes with appeal to the promises
of Moses, keeping the prayer in the orbit of Deuteronomic covenantal theology. In the Chronicler, however, the final verses of
the prayer appeal to the God who sits on the ark in the temple and
alludes to the old war-like summons that mobilizes God to act in

Num 10:35–36. The final appeal is to "your steadfast love for David." The transfer of the appeal *from Moses* (1 Kgs 8:53) *to David* (2 Chr 6:42) is a shift from one tradition to another. It is at the same time a shift from the *bilateral covenant* of Moses to the *unilateral assurance* of David in 2 Sam 7:14–16. Thus, it is an appeal to an assurance that is a more certain and reliable commitment from YHWH that is not dependent on Israel's conduct. The ground for expectation is YHWH's *hesed* (tenacious solidarity). All of these named disasters, including pestilence, are resituated in the orbit of YHWH's steadfast fidelity.

Because the Chronicler's version of Israel's royal history pivots on the temple, we can anticipate that we will have other appeals to the temple as a locus of prayer. We can identify two such variations from the narrative of the books of Kings. In 2 Chr 7:12–16 the narrative has no parallel in the rendition of the books of Kings. In YHWH's second appearance to Solomon in 1 Kgs 9:1–9, there is a general assurance of YHWH's commitment to the temple: "My eyes and my heart will be there for all time" (v. 3). In 2 Chr 7, however, the assurance to the king is much more specific and more extended with reference to the disasters named in the prayer of chapter 6:

> When I shut up the heavens so that there is no rain, or command the locust to devour the land, or send pestilence among my people, if my people who are called by my name humble themselves, pray, seek my face, and turn from their wicked ways, then I will hear from heaven, and will forgive their sin and heal their land. (7:13–14)

Now there is an assurance of being heard and being forgiven. The response of YHWH is an imperative articulated in four verbs that Israel may turn to YHWH: "humble themselves, pray, seek my face, and turn from their evil ways," that is, desist from a way of life that evoked the crisis in the first place (v. 14). This version of God's "second appearance to Solomon is clearly linked to the initial prayer in chapter 6. It amounts to a specific instance of the prayer of chapter 6, thus assuring that the temple is indeed the place of interaction in which YHWH responds to the needs of Israel.

In one more instance, the prayers of Israel in the temple are reported as efficacious in a narrative that has no counterpart in the narrative of Kings. In this narrative account, Jerusalem and King Jehoshaphat are beset by the military threat of the Moabites, Ammonites, and the Edomites; the king in Jerusalem is very much afraid. In response to the crisis, King Jehoshaphat prays to YHWH in the temple (2 Chr 20:6–12). He affirms the "power and might" of YHWH so that "no one is able to stand before you" (v. 6). Anxiously, the king admits that Jerusalem and its army are "powerless" in the face of the threat. Thus, the prayer of the king is framed by the deep contrast between the power of YHWH and the powerlessness of Israel. The prayer concludes:

> O our God, will you not execute judgment upon them?
> For we are powerless against this great multitude that is
> coming against us. We do not know what to do, but our
> eyes are on you. (v. 12)

The eyes of Israel are on YHWH in the temple because there is no alternative help. Where else could Israel look!

In the midst of that encounter, the king voices an approximate quote from the definitive prayer of 2 Chr 6:28, only now the citation ends with an assurance, "YHWH will hear and save" (20:9). The praying king assures that God will rescue. In the subsequent narrative of 20:20–30, the prayer is indeed answered and Jehoshaphat is wondrously rescued from the military threats. It was the Lord who "set an ambush" against Jehoshaphat's enemies. The people had only to pray and sing.

This narrative is one more confirmation of the efficacy of prayer in the Jerusalem temple as the proper resolution of every disaster. The specific case is disaster in war, but the same affirmation applies to every disaster, including pestilence. Indeed in his petition, Jehoshaphat names the three classic disasters—sword, pestilence, and famine (v. 9). In the interaction of prayer and answer, all of the classic threats are reconfigured as accountable to the rule of YHWH.

IDEOLOGY AND MAGICAL THINKING

The text suggests a direct frontal connection between *pestilence and prayer* in ancient Israel. There is no easy way to transfer that connection into our contemporary world. The connection is important enough, however, that we may linger over it. We may wonder what was understood in the circumstance of direct exchange. We may at the outset recognize two dimensions of the connection that do not carry us very far.

First, there is no doubt that the great dedicatory pageant narrative in 1 Kings 8 was in part a staged royal drama with a public relations intent. That is, the promotion of the temple as venue for efficacious prayer served to enhance the monarchy, for the temple was a media engine for the king. It served royal purposes, as the priest Amaziah acknowledged to the prophet Amos (Amos 7:13). The king presided over the people's access to prayer and so managed access to the God of the covenant. There is inescapably a propagandistic element of every state-linked liturgy as we have seen clearly in the president's "prayer breakfast." While this dimension of propaganda does not explain everything, the linkage between power and piety merits close attention.

Second, there is no doubt that some in Israel had a simple-minded notion of prayer as an act of magic whereby the right utterance would deliver the right welcome outcome. Some might anticipate that God could, by fiat, simply wipe away the trouble. And no doubt that same kind of "innocence" about prayer pertains among us whereby proper pious utterance yields good results. Perhaps that innocent theology is evident in the assertion of President Trump that "one day it will disappear . . . like miracle." And of course these texts readily permit such an innocent notion if we are open to such fideism. Utter disregard of scientific evidence suggests that the president might be open to such magical possibility.

41

A RELATIONSHIP THAT
CONTEXTUALIZES DISASTER

We may entertain the thought, however, that beyond propaganda and magic these texts invite and receive a more sophisticated reading by many of the people who framed, transmitted, and cherished these texts. We are not helped at all by any assumption that in a pre-Enlightenment world the people who focused seriously on these texts had such innocence as to read in a simple-minded way.

When we are able to set aside both *propaganda* and *magic,* we are left to consider how these texts are to be understood. We may notice in passing that these texts are quite terse on the disasters themselves, as though they are of no great interest. The texts neither linger to describe the disasters nor do they spend much energy on YHWH's affirmative answer. Rather, the accent is on *faithfulness in uttering the prayer* and *readiness to trust that it will be heard.* That is, the accent is on the effectiveness and reliability of the *relationship that recontextualizes the disaster.*

On the one hand, stress is placed on YHWH's reliable fidelity with reference to either the covenantal promises to Moses (1 Kgs 8:53) or the unilateral promise to David (2 Chr 6:42). The decisive concern is not transactionalism but faithfulness. On the other hand, while Israel is invited to trustful petition, the accent is in turning, repenting, and being humble before YHWH, that is, on re-engaging a loyal way of covenantal existence in response to the purposes of YHWH. When it is recognized that Israel's part is a *restored covenantal life* and YHWH's part is *performance of old promises,* the outcome of such prayer is a reinvigoration of covenantal relationship. It turns out that the several disasters are, in this purview, evocative occasions for the renewal of a life of faith. Israel can continue in trust to hope that YHWH will decisively deal with the disaster, but the accent is elsewhere. It is on the truthfulness and reliability ("grace and truth") of the relationship. As a result, the disaster (war, pestilence, or famine) is rendered penultimate and therefore not life-denying. Israel may indeed hope and trust that threat of pestilence will be overcome. But its energy is devoted to a covenantal life with YHWH.

The Jerusalem temple, as it is imagined in both Kings and Chronicles, is the great dramatic venue for repositioning life in the world. These texts do affirm that good arises when life is lived out in glad obedience to Torah expectations. Such a connection between covenantal life and wellbeing is not excessively innocent. Israel knows that risky dangers persist in God's world. These dangers, however, are not decisive for what is possible or for what is required in the world. Thus war, pestilence, and famine are finally seen as accountable to the creator God, who presides even over such disasters. Virus is thereby robbed of its capacity to disorder daily life. In effect, these texts decisively *change the subject* from disaster to the rule of YHWH. Such a changed subject revises how we may live in the neighborhood when it is under threat.

The Giver of Bread and Fish

(Matthew 7:7–11)

We do "thoughts and prayers" easily and glibly;
    we do "thoughts" without thinking;
    we do "prayers" without praying.
We commit that glib act
    because it is what we know how to do with an anemic god, or
    because we are embarrassed to do more, or
    because it is convenient and costs us nothing.
Now, however, we are driven to *unthinkable thoughts*, about
    all that is ending, and
    all this we have lost, and
    all that leaves us with a sinking feeling.
Now, however, we are driven, some of us, to *unutterable prayers*.
    We are driven to such prayer
        by awareness that our usual reliabilities are gone.
    We are driven to you, the abiding God
        when other helpers fail and comforts flee.
Thus we are bold to pray:
    We are bold to *ask*, because it will be given!
        So we pray for the end of the virus,
            for the health of the neighborhood,
            for the recovery of the economy.
    We are bold to *seek*, because you will be found!
        We seek your mercy and your goodness and your
        generosity,
            so let yourself be found by us.
    We are bold to *knock*, because it will be opened.
        We know many doors slammed shut,
        doors of health and safety and comfort and fun.
        Open to us the door of life, and love, and peace, and joy.
Here we are in your presence:
    We ask for *bread:*
        the bread of life,
        the bread of abundance,
        the bread of neighborly sharing.
        Do not give us a stone or a crumb.
    We ask for *fish:*

the fish of a good diet,
the fish of your abundant waters,
the fish that signs the gospel.
Do not give us a snake or the hiss of poison.
We dare to pray, not because we are at our wits end,
but because you are at the center of our life.
Our hope is in no other save in thee alone!
So hear, heal, save, restore!
Be the God you have promised to be. Amen.

5

THE "TURN" FROM SELF TO GOD

Psalm 77

Psalm 77 offers a stunning embodiment of the reorientation of life most hoped for by evangelical faith. In the exposition that follows, I take the psalm not simply as a devotional or liturgical residue of faith but as an actual "speech pilgrimage" of one whose self spoke through to new faith. Specifically, the psalm shows the route by which this life was moved from a *preoccupation with self* to a *submission to and reliance upon God*.

SELF-CONCERN

The first part of the psalm is a fairly standard lament statement.[1] We can enter its claim by noticing the quite different rhetorical moves made by the speaker.

1. The speaker is turned in on self in pity and self-preoccupation, and they can speak of nothing but self (vv. 1–6):

> *I* cry aloud to God . . .
> *I* seek the Lord

1. See Brueggemann, *Praying the Psalms*, 8–11; *Spirituality of the Psalms*, 25–45.

46

my hand is stretched out,
my soul refuses to be comforted.
I think of God,
I moan
I meditate,
   my spirit faints,
   my eyelids are kept by God from closing
I am so troubled that *I* cannot speak
I consider the days of old,
I remember the years of long ago,
I commune with *my heart*[2]
I meditate and search *my spirit.*

The speaker does a complete inventory of his/her own person and sees how it is all, in every part, mobilized for self-concern.[3]

2. Then in vv. 7–9, there is a series of rhetorical questions. But even here there is no yielding of the agenda of self:

Will the Lord spurn forever
   and never again be favorable?
Has steadfast love ceased forever?
   Are his promises at an end for all time?
Has God forgotten to be gracious?
   Has he in anger shut up his compassion?

There is obviously a reference to YHWH, more than appeared in vv. 1–6. But the rhetorical effort is to draw YHWH completely into the orbit of self-concern. In these verses, there occur three of Israel's most precious covenantal words, *hesed, hanan, raham*—loyalty, graciousness, compassion. The questions pose the most urgent faith issues. They ask about the very character of God. But they are questions that emerge out of an overriding self-concern. They appear to ask about God's faithfulness. But they really ask, what about me? Even the most primal qualities of YHWH are consumed in this self-preoccupation. Thus far, we are at the pool

---

2. "I commune with my heart" is a statement of religion reduced to self-preoccupation, not unlike the characterization of the Pharisee (Luke 18:11) who "prayed with himself."

3. The self-inventory is paralleled to the lamentation of Ps 22:17: "I count all my bones."

of Narcissus.[4] The speaker sounds as one who understands how it all works. He knows what mobilizes God's *hesed* and *raham*. She knows how to get to it. The crisis of the poem may be one of two things. Either the speaker knows how to make it all work, which means everything has been emptied of mystery, or, more likely, even though the speaker knows how to make it work, it does not work! It is then a religion that has failed.

Janzen has suggested that some rhetorical questions in the speech of the Old Testament are not mere rhetoric but are serious questions.[5] Such questions ask the unaskable. In the form of a question, the speaker moves into dangerous and unexplored territory in the space between us and the throne. In our psalm, the speaker is a person of conventional obedience. He has some ground to stand on and some legitimate expectations of YHWH. He is not a renegade who has forfeited his expectations from God. But the voice of obedience is on the move, driven there by the failure of convention. Her imagination is beginning to move, beginning to guess that God's *hesed* is not unilaterally unconditional and automatically linked to this particular believer. The poem begins to suspect that God's *hesed* (if indeed God is faithful!) has other worlds to work and cannot be summoned on demand. God is not on call. There is a probe here that the space between the two partners is dangerous and unknown. All of that space has not yet been reduced and routinized so that it can be presumed upon. Some of the space between here and God's throne is untamed and therefore unpredictable. And if the space is beyond control, it makes one more frantically press for the old, innocent faith that had God encapsulated.

This speaker had grown comfortable with the great affirmations of YHWH because the great affirmations readily translated

4. Christopher Lasch has made important linkages between the myth and the pathology of our time in *Culture of Narcissism: American Life in an Age of Diminishing Expectations*. One of the important ingredients in such immobilizing narcissism is the flattening of imagination so that the person is incapable of thinking of life other than it presently is, or incapable of thinking of life beyond self.

5. Janzen, "Metaphor and Reality in Hosea 11."

into self-serving assurance. But now that is all being blown out of the water. A God who has been reduced to the safe proposals of "a torah so righteous" (cf. Deut 4:8) is now known to be a God whose "form is not seen" (cf. Deut 4:12), even if that form is thought to consist in *hesed, hanan, raham*. The desperate rhetorical questions appear in vv. 7–9 after this self-inventory of vv. 1–6. The speaker begins to guess that the old, sure religion is collapsing.

NEW QUESTIONS

There is a striking move from the "I, I, I," in vv. 1–6, which is still safely rooted and conventional and with no failure of nerve, to the probe of the questions of vv. 7–9, which ask new questions. And then there is v. 10. This verse is the crucial turn in the psalm, exceedingly difficult to translate. This verse clearly looks both ways, back to the "I" statements of vv. 1–6 and forward to the rest of the psalm (vv. 11–20). Verse 10 consists in two elements. The first element is a statement about *grief or trouble.*[6] The second element is a statement of *change*, presumably that God has changed. The translation is difficult, and there is some variation of nuance. RSV renders:

> And I say, "It is my grief
> that the right hand of the Most High has changed."

The Jerusalem Bible renders:

> "This," I said then, "is what distresses me;
> that the power of the Most High is no longer what it was."

More poignantly, the New English Bible renders:

> Has his right hand, I said, lost its grasp?
> Does it hang powerless, the arm of the Most High?

Kraus comments: "God's works and ways are for human beings out of reach (Isa 55:8ff); they lie in an inaccessible,

---

6. Calvin, *Commentary on the Book of Psalms*, 2:214–15, takes the word from *hlh*, and understands it as "kill" (pierce), and renders it "my death." See the helpful and lucid comment of Anderson, *Book of Psalms*, 2:558.

consuming brightness. He himself, YHWH, is the Holy One (Pss 71:22, 89:19[ET=18]), the 'wholly Other.' His salvific deeds prove his incomparability (cf. Exod 15:11)."[7]

The speaker has discovered that YHWH has freedom, will not be on call, not presumed upon. God is not locked into a quid pro quo. And it causes grief, illness, despondency to discern that the partner has changed. Observance of the freedom God has to change causes a terrible unsettling among the faithful. The sure comfort of an utterly obedient relationship is shattered by the awareness that this hidden, free God will not be fully discerned or completely predictable. And the response must be to break out of obedience of a simple kind for the practice of an imagination that seeks to find other ways of relating to this free God. To relate to such a free God requires freedom on the part of the believer, a freedom likely censored by the conventional religion of vv. 1–6.

The grief here expressed is not unlike the pouting of Jonah over God's graciousness (Jonah 4:1, 9). Only here, the depression is more intense. And the substance moves in the opposite direction from that of Jonah. Jonah is disconcerted that God is gracious when he does not want God to be gracious. Here the psalmist is dismayed that God is not graciousness when he had fully counted on that predictable graciousness.

The discernment of Ps 77:10, anguished as it is, admits of more than one reading. If one is linked to a flat, one-dimensional faith, then this verse is *a bitter loss of faith*. But if we think in terms of obedience on its way to risky imagination, then this verse is *an opening for new faith* beyond the conventions and routines that secure but do not reckon with God's *awefulness*. This verse stands at a very risky and dangerous place where evangelical faith often stands. And indeed must stand. And as we stand there, we never know in advance if we face *loss of faith* or *opening for new faith*. The dramatic substance of v. 10 leaves the issue quite unresolved. And we must not rush past that dramatic moment in this speech-pilgrimage.

7. Kraus, *Psalms 60–150*, 116.

A WOUNDED PARTNER

So the psalm makes its desperate way beyond v. 10. We have now the speech of a wounded partner well beyond the old innocence. We do not know how this speaker moves from v. 10 to v. 11. But we can surmise it was not an easy move. We do not know how any faith-speaker makes the leap from the preoccupation with self to an imaginative acknowledgment of the primacy of the other. But that is what happens in this psalm and in all serious biblical faith. It involves leaving the safety of "the torah so righteous" for "the God so near" who is yet so free (Deut 4:7–8). The dramatic move concerns the abandonment of self as the primal agenda for the Thou who is out beyond us in freedom. And we make no mistake to observe that that transfer of the agenda, that ceding of concern for self to the other, is the crucial move of biblical faith, the *sine qua non* for covenanting. And we observe what an urgent, difficult task Christian nurture and preaching now is. For the narcissism of our culture (on which see vv. 1–6) is precisely aimed at *not* ceding self, not relinquishing. This psalm models the very move of faith that our cultural ideology wants to prevent. The whole consumer perspective concerns retention of self and satiation of self. That is what is given in vv. 1–6, and what is relinquished in what follows.

Note that this was not the only move possible after v. 10. It is one among some options. After the wonderment of the questions of vv. 7–9 and the startling discovery of v. 10, another move could have been made. The speaker could have moved to Ps 14 and concluded, "There is no God." The move beyond v. 10 is a hazardous one—for any of us. And the outcome is never sure ahead of time. But the move has been made here, a move that now reckons the free "Thou" as the starting point for life.[8]

---

8. Worth noting is the argument made here in sharp distinction from that of Gordon Kaufman in his excellent book, *Theological Imagination*, 63–75. If I read Kaufman correctly, he argues that the self-conscious assertion of "I" leads to the liberating reality of "Thou." I believe this psalm argues that the move is not from a full act of self-consciousness but from relinquishment of self, precisely what modernity finds so difficult.

51

That move, one of several possibilities, concerns us directly as we seek to be faithful and as we seek to live in our culture. On the one hand, that move made in v. 11 is a move from a religion of law to a religion of grace. It articulates the awareness that we live by gift and not by grasp. On the other hand, observe that in our society of consumer narcissism, a *religion of petty moralistic obedience* goes with an *economics of satiation*. That is, in our secularized version of it, we do not hope for God to satisfy all our desires (Ps 145:16). But we do expect to have all our desires satisfied, even if by another source. So we are part of a culture that holds together *consumer satiation* and *petty obedience*. That tight alliance serves to keep *us* as the agenda, an excuse for not ceding life beyond self, an inability to transfer attention beyond our needs and appetites.

The religious temptation among us is to walk close to the dangerous rhetorical questions of vv. 7–9 and become aware of the hurt and anguish of v. 10 but then not move on to v. 11, not move to the "Thou," but to circle back again to vv. 1–6, which permits a preoccupation with self (and self's program) and requires a numbing.[9] Because being numb will do if there is no deliverance.

A NEW WORLD OF IMAGINATION

By the mercy of God, the psalm does not circle back. And if it did, it would then be only a mirror for our fearful self-preoccupation. It would then not be a model of faith but only an exercise in self-serving. But it moves on. It says something new and surprising and unpredictable. And that is why we attend to it. It moves on in remarkable fashion so that v. 11 follows closely after v. 10. We may be glad for that modeling of the move. But we recognize at the same time that we do not know how it is possible. We presume that this move, here or anywhere, is not made easily or quickly. Likely, there is a long pause in the psalm, a desperate resistance, a

9. On "numbing" as the problem of our culture, see Dorothee Soelle, *Suffering*; and especially the important work of Robert J. Lifton, whose major summary is *The Broken Connection*.

counting the cost, like standing at the edge of the cold swimming pool, testing it with a toe, putting it off, and then the quantum leap into the new icy world of imaginative faith. It is indeed a turning loose of the old self.

The move from vv. 1–10 to v. 11 is like the move envisioned by Jesus:

> For whoever would save his life will lose it;
> and whoever loses his life for my sake
> and the gospel's will save it. (Mark 8:35)

The first part, with the series of "I" is about *keeping life*. And the move to the second part with the series of "Thou" is a readiness to *lose life in order to gain it*. I do not suggest that prayer and liturgy are the full scope of self-surrender. But I am very sure that unless there are liturgic ways for that move in our lives, we will not make them elsewhere, either with reference to personal maturation or to social change. The very rhetoric of Israel here makes such a move thinkable, i.e., capable of being imagined.

There is a waiting, a hoping, a resisting, a yielding, a dying, a being surprised. By v. 11, the speaker has abandoned the preoccupation with self and is able to focus on this one who "has changed," the same change that caused resentment and loss in v. 10.

Re-entering Our Past

By v. 11, the speaker is on the way into a new world of imagination. In vv. 1–6, the speaker had focused narrowly on "my present," which is all consuming. Now there is a reentry into "our past," which had been bracketed out in self-preoccupation. And in the pondering of that past, the speaker comes to the fresh awareness that it is precisely God's freedom to change and come and go that is the hope of Israel and the deliverance of folks like the speaker, in this present or in any present.

In the second part of the psalm, a very different vocabulary is now at work:

v. 11   "deeds" (*ma'alele*)
       "wonders" (*pil'ekah*)
v. 12   "work" (*pa'alekah*)
       "deeds" (*'alilothikah*)

These four terms are stated in a concise chiasmus. The key point is made in v. 13: "Thy way, O God, is holy (*qadosh*)." God's way is "wholly Other" (*ganz Anders*), not to be reduced, not to be accommodated or conformed either to my needs or my expectations. And then, following naturally, there is an assertion of incomparability: "What god is great like our God?" The question sounds like that of Deut 4:8, to which we have made reference. No god like ours, no god so near, no god so free, no god so surprising or exasperating. Here is the end to all analogy. And the bold, liberated speaker of vv. 11–20 discovers that the self-preoccupied speaker of vv. 1–6 was complaining about an idol, for this free God of *hesed, hanan, raham* will not be treated like a fortune cookie.

A Concluding Recontextualization

The remainder of the psalm (vv. 15–20) is like a credo that recites the great deeds of the past. Verse 15 uses Exodus language with the verb *ga'al*. Verses 16–18 talk about a storm. It could be any storm God. The language is not unlike the Canaanite imagery of Ps 29. But the language of the storm is regularly drawn toward this people. Verse 16 has echoes of Ps 114:3–4, which uses sea imagery for Exodus. Verses 17–18 are about a storm. But the point is for Israel in vv. 19–20, which becomes completely concrete and completely Israelite at the end, with the mention of Moses and Aaron.

Most striking about this psalm is its abrupt ending. Nothing here about a return to the agenda of vv. 1–6. There is nothing about all of that being resolved. It is as though the speaker is left to draw her own conclusions about the condition of vv. 1–6 in relation to the statements of vv. 15–20. Nothing has been resolved, but everything has been recontextualized. The speaker in vv. 1–6 is preoccupied because he is caught in a narrow range in which such personal trouble requires a conclusion that God does not care.

That narrow religious agenda is however shattered. It is shattered by remembering, by awareness of God's incomparability, by reference to Israel's concrete history, but most of all, it is shattered by the utterance, *Thou* (*'attah*).

Now I have dealt with this psalm in detail because I take it to be structurally the story of God's people who are always *trapped* and/or *on the move*. This psalm knows that all of us live in this battle. We struggle to stay home with the sure company of "I." We move between a petty religion of calculating obedience aimed at well-being and a fully-liberated, imaginative religion of awe and amazement and trembling before the Holy One. In this psalm, vv. 1–6 (7–9) articulate the first; vv. 11–20 speak about the alternative. The first is dominated by "I." The second is governed by "Thou."

> *Thou* art God (v. 14)
> *Thou* didst redeem thy people with *thine* own arm (v. 15)
> the waters saw *thee*
> the crash of *thy* thunder
> *thy* lightnings
> *thy* way was through the sea
> *thy* path through the great waters
> *thy* footprints unseen (vv. 16–19).
> *Thou* didst lead thy people (v. 20).

Note that after v. 12, there is not a single "I." One can observe that there is a neat contrast between the "my" of the first half—my trouble, my hand, my spirit, my eyelids, my soul, my heart, my spirit—and the "thy" in the second half—thy thunder, thy lightning, thy way, thy path, thy footprints. The rhetorical change cannot be accidental. The contrast is total, decisive, and intentional. And the turn is in v. 10. Everything is up for grabs in v. 10, waiting for fresh resolution. It is the pastoral moment that could go either way. It is the evangelical moment in which the news may break. It is a moment of deciding to live in the world where the Most High changes or to retreat back into a world where "least high" keeps us at the center of things. It is the pastoral task to be present to that moment of terror, a moment which requires enormous imagination.

∾

From Self to Thou

You, holy, faithful, merciful God,
    have called us into being,
    given us names, faces, and vocations, and
    we live them out in freedom.
In our freedom, we notice only sometimes, that
    we cannot cope with all that comes at us,
    we cannot finally outflank the forces that address us, and
    we cannot by ourselves deal with the grief, trouble, and anger
    that well up in us.
After our imagined autonomy,
    we gladly turn back to you.
After we have said "I" for a very long time,
    we fall back to "Thou";
        we utter the "Thou" who inhabits our memories,
            memories of rescue, healing, and forgiveness;
        we utter the "thou" who occupies our best hopes,
            as we hope for peace, wellbeing, and justice in the
            world.
We move back into faithful dialogue with you:
    we say "thou" as we thank and praise you;
    we say "I" as we act out our freedom and accept our
    responsibility.
Just now, in the face of the virus, we find our best "I" without force,
    and so we say "thou,"
        "thou" in power,
        "thou" in mercy,
        "thou" in faithfulness,
            finally "Thou"!
We remember all your wonders, and then, in gladness,
    we remember who we are as yours;
    we recover our gratitude, our hope, our resolve, and our confidence. Amen.

6

GOD'S NEW THING

Isaiah 43:18–19

It is possible to trust that the God of the Gospel is in, with, and under the crisis of the virus without imagining that God is the cause of it. As God often does, in hidden ways God may be amid this crisis to do the hard work of checking arrogance and curbing hubris. Amid the virus, we now face an alert about the indifferent, exploitative world of global self-sufficiency we have been making and that some of us mightily enjoy.

— We now see curbed the absolute world of technological certitude that faces a mystery beyond calculation.

— We see that our immense power is unable to fend off a threat that is for the moment beyond our explanation.

— We see that our great wealth is not able to assure us of security.

We are pressed back to basics!

The God of the Gospel, however, not only curbs and checks our excessive ambition. We may imagine God doing a new thing among us. Perhaps we are arriving at a new neighborly normal:

— Imagine, we are treating prisoners differently, even releasing some who constitute no threat.

— Imagine, we are mobilizing generous financing for needy neighbors who must have resources in order to survive.

— Imagine, we are finding generous provisions for students and their debts.

In the assertion of God's newness, the prophet is engaged in a daring act of imagination whereby he hosts a possible world that is not yet in view. If we are to be faithful heirs and practitioners of this daring prophetic imagination then we, too, in the wake of the prophet, are summoned to engage in daring imagination concerning new historical possibility. The heirs of the prophetic tradition are not captured by what they see in front of them. Nor are they smitten by a preoccupation with what once was treasured. Prophetic imagination is the anticipation of new social possibility that is available from the intention of the God of the prophets. What is now required of us is not simply fantasy but moral imagination to express historical possibility that is congruent with God's hope for neighborliness. That moral imagination is rooted in promise; at the same time, it is grounded in the realities of dollars, laws, natural resources, and social conditions. The prophetic task is to submit our awareness of dollars, laws, natural resources, and social conditions to the hopes of the creator God. Such imagination is indeed, "The assurance of things hoped for and the conviction of things not seen" (Heb 11:1).

In our moment of fear and insecurity, we may be tempted to hold on to what was once safe and secure. Prophetic tradition knows, to the contrary, that the future does not reside in old, treasured realities. It belongs, rather, to bold faithful thought that evokes bold faithful action. This has always been the prophetic task, and it is now, in this freighted moment, our prophetic task. The new thing God is making possible is a world of generous, neighborly compassion. It is before our very eyes! The God who does this new thing has also said, "Do not remember former things." We have so much we will do well to forget:

— We may forget punitive measures toward outliers.

— We may forget parsimony toward those in need.

— We may forget predatory policies toward the vulnerable.

The good news is that we need not go back to those old ways that are punitive, parsimonious, and predatory. We can embrace a new normal that is God's gift to us!

At the Edge of a New Normal

Our "normal ways" are reassuring to us:
>It is our normal way to slot people for wealth or poverty;
>It is our normal way to classify people as "us" and "other";
>It is our normal way to prefer males to the other gender;
>It is our normal way to distinguish heteros and the "other."

Our usual normals make us safe,
>make us happy,
>leave us certain.

Only now our normal ways are exposed as constructs of privilege
that cover over the reality of our neighborly situation.
In the midst of the virus we notice that the others are very much
with us,
>and we are all vulnerable together.

We sense the disruption, the loss, the deep dis-ease among us,
>and we want our old normals to be "great again."

Except that we cannot!
Except that you summon us to new futures made sober by the
pandemic;
>You require us now to imagine, to risk, and be vulnerable
>>as we watch the new normals emerge among us:
>>>the blind see, lepers are cleansed, the poor have good
>>>news;
>>>students have debts canceled, the poor have health
>>>care,
>>>workers have a living wage, the atmosphere breathes
>>>fresh air.

We want to return to the old normals that yield (for some) safety and
happiness,
>but you dispatch us otherwise.

Your new normal for us requires some adjustment by us.
>And adjust we will. We will live and trust and share differently.

"All things new" is a huge stretch for us.
But we know it is your good gift to us; with wistfulness, we receive it
>we embrace it, and
>we give thanks to you. Amen.

7

THE MATRIX OF GROAN

Isaiah 42:14–15

The phrase "all creation is groaning" is employed by Paul in Rom 8:22 wherein he elaborates on the struggle for newness through the anguish and demand of labor pains, a new creation willed by God but not yet birthed, only in anticipation. My modest comment is that we must not pass over the labor pains, cries, and demands too readily. My colleague tells of a time of a characteristically demanding birth process in an earlier day in his family, when the father was, as usual, not present in the hospital at the birth. Soon after the birth, the father hurried to the hospital and reassured his weary wife and new mother, "Well, that wasn't so bad, was it?" Even though he is often accused of being a sexist, Paul was under no illusion about the problematic nature of birth pangs—how deep, how painful, how nearly unbearable they may be.

We do not know from whence Paul drew his insight, but perhaps like every male interpreter short on such an actual experience, he learned from a text. Long before Paul, the poet of the Isaiah tradition has God say:

> For a long time I have held my peace,
> I have kept still and restrained myself;

now I will cry out like a woman in labor,
     I will gasp and pant.
I will lay waste mountains and hills,
     and dry up all their herbage. (Isa 42:14–15)

Under this imagery, newness is never cozy; it arrives through a struggle that turns out to be birth, though along the way the struggle might have been mistaken for death pangs. Newness is not easy for the God who will create a homecoming for exiles, according to this poet. Newness is not easy in creation that is too long in the grip of deathliness. *The process* of newness, perhaps not sufficiently considered in this book, is a process of pain that is very deep, so deep that it cannot be lived through quietly or serenely, perhaps not by either the creator or by the creation.

NOT KEEPING SILENT

The people of God in the Isaiah in this text (or in the Romans text) are, of course, not strangers to the groan of protest and anguish. God's creation and all of the creatures are not intended for abuse and suffering; for that reason there is something innate to human creatures in the image of God, something innate to God's people as God's partners, and something innate in creation itself as God's beloved world that will not keep silent in the process of dying and receiving new life. The texts of such anguished groaning that occurred to me include the following: "What have you done? Listen; your brother's blood is crying out to me from the ground!" (Gen 4:10). The old world of death is accomplished by Cain, but the dead Abel is not finished. The cry of Abel is a cry for vindication, a cry of pain about violence and, we dare say, a groaning toward the resurrection of life to be given again. The cry may be only in the ears of Cain and may be only on the lips of murdered Abel. For our purposes, however, it is important that the cry is "from the ground" (*min-haʾadamah*), the very ground that constitutes the bottom layer of creation (see Gen 2:5, 9; 3:17; 4:21–23; 5:29; 8:21). The ground is not only the scene for and witness to human violence but also the endless carrier of the residue of violence that brings anguish to the earth that remains blood-soaked.

Israelites Groaned under Slavery

> After a long time the king of Egypt died. The Israelites groaned under their slavery, and cried out. Out of the slavery their cry for help rose up to God. (Exod 2:23)

How incredible that the Exodus narrative does not begin—as Calvinists are wont to say—with divine initiative. It begins rather with Israel "groaning and crying out" in the burden of oppression that has become unbearable for the slaves. Now, beyond Genesis 4, this cry is historical and is not directly a cry of creation; except, as Terence Fretheim has shown, the moves of Pharaoh against Israel and the responses of YHWH to Pharaoh's chaos-enactment deeply impinge upon the created order.[1] The plagues are actions of the creator in response to the groans of Israel for newness. We could readily imagine that the Nile, for example, could join the cry of the Hebrew slaves, for the Nile is soon to be taken up into Pharaoh's anxious deathliness (see Exod 7:14–25). The groan of Israel surely echoes around the Egyptian territory that is almost usurped from the legitimate hand of YHWH into alien, chaotic governance.[2]

The Land Cried Out

> If my land has cried out against me,
>   and its furrows have wept together;
> if I have eaten its yield without payment,
>   and caused the death of its owners;
> let thorns grow instead of wheat,
>   and foul weeds instead of barley.
>   (Job 31:38–40)

---

1. Fretheim, "Plagues as Ecological Signs." See also Brueggemann, "Theme Revisited: Bread Again!"

2. See Brueggemann, "Pharaoah as Vassal."

It is astonishing that Job's long recital of innocence—taken often to be the acme of Israelite ethics—culminates with an ecological affirmation. Indeed, the recital seems to culminate in vv. 35-37, Job's defiant challenge to his accuser. The statement of innocence seems concluded in those verses, except that Job reaches rhetorically for one more extreme assertion of innocence. He claims that he has been environmentally responsive, a claim that makes even all his preceding neighbor claims penultimate. Job knows well that land—since it is blood-soaked by Abel—can groan, anguish, and cry out. The good news is that Job's ecological commitments have caused the land, in this case, to be satisfied. The earth has not accused Job in angry thorns of protest or in enraged weeds of vengeance. The text tells negatively about the groan that has not been required or uttered. In our context of ecology, however, one may more fully appreciate Job's innocence, for his care for the earth has made the groan of earth unnecessary.[3]

The Stones Would Shout

Some of the Pharisees in the crowd said to him, "Teacher, order your disciples to stop." He answered, "I tell you, if these were silent, the stones would shout out."
(Luke 19:39-40)

The text does not, to be sure, concern a cry of anguish; the NRSV nicely renders the Greek noun *krazousin* as "shout out." The potential of stones "shouting out" is in case the crowds of disciples in v. 38 do not exuberantly shout out a welcome to the king who comes in the name of the Lord. The shouting disciples welcome the newness embodied by Jesus, newness that the Pharisees want to stop and do not welcome. But non-human creation is perfectly capable of sounding the exuberance in case human exuberance fails (see also Ps 96:1-13 on the creation welcoming the new, coming king). The context indicates shout and not groan. But notice

---

3. The work of Wendell Berry is especially pertinent on this point. See, for example, his *The Gift of the Good Land*. See also Dempsey and Butkus, *All Creation Is Groaning*.

that the same verb can readily mean a cry of anguish; in any case, the welcome shout is an eager longing for newness because the old has failed.

These four texts are representative of the world of *cry/shout/ groan*, the world of *anguish and expectation* in which the groan of Romans 8 is situated. The new creation does not come easily, but only in a painful struggle that is both anguish and hope.

THE COMING OF NEW CREATION

I have taken this long with these texts that belong to the same semantic field as the groan of Romans 8 because I want to consider the groan of pain and the shout of hope that belong to the coming of new creation. The future, so claims biblical faith, is not an easy, convenient gift; it is not an automatic "next" that comes in "progress." It is not a neat technological accomplishment akin to the solving of a puzzle. It is rather a mystery-shrouded gift of God that all the creatures are invited to receive in deep cost. Thus, the theological-liturgical-pastoral question of the groan of newness looms large and permits no easy solution.

From God's side, I suppose, new creation will come as God chooses. But the coming of new creation is with an ethical passion that requires us to consider the groan of newness from a human side. The truth of newness from the human side is that God's gift comes at huge cost, the cost of acknowledging that old creation has failed and is dysfunctional, the awareness that new creation requires disciplined, intentional reception. As a result, the move from old to new entails bewildering loss of control that comes in relinquishment. The move from an old creation marked by rapacious acquisitiveness to the new world of justice, mercy, compassion, peace, and security is one that in socio-economic, political terms necessitates renunciation, repentance, yielding, and ceding of what has been. The move calls to mind the old question of baptism that in a therapeutic culture sounds so harsh, "Do you now renounce Satan and all his works?"—a renunciation of the economic, political dimension that will be experienced as deep loss and will evoke deep groans of a quite concrete, practical kind. Indeed, the depth of relinquishment is not unlike the Pauline structure of baptism in Romans 6, so we might hear the groan of Romans 8 already anticipated in the baptism of Romans 6:

> What then are we to say? Should we continue in sin in order that grace may abound? By no means! How can we who died to sin go on living in it? Do you not know that all of us who have been baptized into Christ Jesus were baptized into his death? Therefore we have been buried with him by baptism into death, so that, just as Christ was raised from the dead by the glory of the Father, so we too might walk in newness of life. For if we have been united with him in a death like his, we will certainly be united with him in a resurrection like his. We know that our old self was crucified with him, so that the body of sin might be destroyed, and we might no longer be en-slaved to sin. For whoever has died is freed from sin. But if we have died with Christ, we believe that we will also live with him. (Rom 6:1–8)

The groan is that mark of shock, bewilderment, and recognition that stands between the old world of death and the new world of life. That moment between, Paul understands well, cannot be eluded but is the narrow entry point into new creation. The groan is the gate to the future of God's new creation.

A Groan without a Future

I can imagine *a groan without a future*, a relinquishment in which there are no new gifts and no new creation, because the new cre-ation is only promised but not guaranteed. In a modern/post mod-ern world so deeply secular, one can at least entertain the thought that the religious claim of newness is romanticism and there is, in fact, no Giver behind the expected gift of newness. Such a thought is, of course, well outside the scope of this book and outside the scope of faith that propels the book, but that edge of potential *de-spair* is there and it is real. In the midst of our great advocacies of

newness and our modest relinquishments of what is old, there is
the deep threat of despair that there will be no new creation. That
despair, moreover, I judge, is not simply out there but inside the
household of faith. Our talk of new creation might on occasion be
a bit too facile in our buoyancy.

A Future without Groan

But my real intention is to invert that proposition, not groan without
a future but *a future without groan*—or, as Christian liturgy might
suggest, Easter Sunday without Good Friday. In a therapeutic culture in which reality is too soon reduced to entertainment, there
is a ready attempt to eliminate the groan, to imagine that one can
get from old to new, from death to life, in easy fashion without the
pangs of death or of birth. That is, the ideology of the global economy and its match in buoyant religious affirmation are, in deep ways,
an act of denial, a practice of getting from there to here without any
acknowledgment of the trouble or trauma or the cost of newness.
It is known among us that the new creation, from the human side,
is a new network of care that requires the end of domination and
exploitation, the end of controlling truth and monopolies of certitude, the end of an oil-based comfort that makes every day one of
ease, comfort, luxury, extravagance, and self-indulgence. That new
network of care depends upon a willingness to think of creation not
only as wondrous gift but also as uncompromising limit.

The groan might be the loud, unrequited blood of Abel, the
unbearable slavery of Egypt, an uncared for field envisioned by
Job, or an exuberant welcome from a rock (stone) concert. But the
groan of new creation might also be on the lips of privileged West-
erners over the loss of SUVs, academics on the loss of new technol-
ogies, or taxpayers over the loss of easy accumulation. We should
not remove the cosmic groan from the real life of creatureliness,
for we have known autonomy and deeply resent the accounting
to which the creator summons in the emergence of newness. Thus
I suggest that we might reflect on the liturgical, artistic, political,

economic, scientific dimension of the groan that awaits us. For the cycles of denial can only be broken among us by the truth of groan.

Educated for Relinquishment and Renunciation

The fact is that uncritical, systemic affluence that issues in consumerism is an incredible narcotic that keeps us in the grip of old creation and its deathliness. Under such a narcotic, we remain unschooled in hearing groans from non-human creatures, unaccustomed to deep human heaving. Under such a narcotic, critical discussion is too trivialized by therapists, managers, and entertainers; sex, power, money, and security become the defining marks of systemic denial. The cry characteristically breaks the vicious cycles of denial. But the cry will be put off for as long as we can. In this moment of crisis and denial, education for relinquishment and renunciation is essential if we are to hear the groan and if we are to resist saying in our unnoticing, "Well, that wasn't so bad." It is, as Paul might have said in the depth of groan, now very bad—very glorious in prospect—but now very bad.

The Exile and the Cross

The twin habits of *denial* that refuses to groan in acknowledgment of a failed creation and *despair* that groans but entertains no prospect of newness after the groan are practices that preclude newness; for without groan, there is no birth of newness; without hope, there is no move out of groan. Of course, new creation will be God's utter gift among us, but it is a gift given only where old creation is groaned and relinquished in expectation. Creation's groan cannot of itself bring newness, but that groan is surely a human *sine qua non* for its coming. And if a prerequisite is creation's groan in birth pangs, then the human creature, the creature who has most misunderstood our assigned role in creation, must do most of the groan. The human creature is deepest into the dysfunction of old creation and so must groan. The human creature is

68

peculiarly gifted by God, so the human creature must be the hoper for the reception of a new creation.

If we look for models of the groan that will break the despair and the cry that will override the denial, we may look in two places in Scripture that provide clues about where to look in life. First, the proper practice of hope for newness in the Old Testament, including "new heavens, new earth, new Jerusalem" in Isa 65:17–25, is *the exile*. Exile—the brokenness of things past—is the context for such hope. Moreover, all of that hope in ancient Israel is after the book of Lamentations, that is, past the large, public, loud groan.

In parallel fashion, in the New Testament it is the voice of Friday from *the cross* that does the groan that opens the way to Easter newness. The cry of Ps 22:1, on the lips of Jesus, from the cross, in abandonment, is the narrative-liturgical acknowledgment that even Messiah, the bodied hope for newness, must receive newness in the exile. Only when we, hopers for new creation, disown our present dysfunction in its deathliness and dare to voice a groan that matches God's birthing of newness, only then will God give.

I accent groan because the force of evolutionary development, just now in the form of globalization, readily believes in new creation at the "End of History." But that new creation, on the wings of technological progress, is a lie. The newness of God is not given in self-congratulatory buoyancy but in the candor and hope of those who receive what they cannot conjure for themselves. This biblical insistence is not a picture of pessimism; rather, it is a counter-argument against rational optimism that will not wait long enough in the absence. It is in the absence that the newness comes. And so the task of faithful, candid, expectant imagination is to give absence full play, to give groan full sound. Those who do so may be among the first fruits of the spirit who groans inwardly while we wait for adoption, the redemption of our bodies. If it were easier than that or less costly than that, we would not be into birth pangs but into serene maturity with no pangs and without anguish. But we are only at the pangs. Nobody will say about such candor and hope, "Well, that wasn't so bad, was it?"

∽

A Thou Who Hears!

We prefer our worship of you should be upbeat.
We like it that the church is "the happiest place in town."
We take our glimpse or your promised kingdom as a venue,
  where never is heard
  a discouraging word! .
But then . . . reality!!
  like suffering and death,
  like pandemic and virus,
  like loss unimaginable!
That reality breaks our happy illusion of a fairy-tale life in the first
world,
  and we are left with stone-cold fear and
      bottomless need.
So we cry out with urgent imperative:
  Hear, help, save!!
  We cry out along with the whole company of people of faith
  who have cried out.
  We cry out, because our cry, since the lips of the slaves in Egypt,
      is our most elemental word back to you, our creator.
  We cry out, not in despair, but in confidence that you hear.
You are the one, the only one, who can turn sorrow to joy,
          mourning to dancing,
          weeping to laughter.
So now, God who hears, helps, and saves,
  hear, act, and make new!
      Give us courage and patience;
      end the virus;
      let us be rich in soul and poor in things,
      ordered for neighborliness,
      generous with goods,
      free of fear,
          but mostly: end the virus!
We pray this in the name of Jesus who defeated the powers of death,
  overcame the forces of evil,
      ended the unbearable vexation of leprosy for some, and
      became the Lord of the Dance.

the dance of wellbeing, gladness, and peace.
So we pray,
so we trust,
so we hope . . . in you! Amen.

BIBLIOGRAPHY

Anderson, A. A. *Book of Psalms.* 2 vols. New Century Bible. London: Oliphant, 1972.

Barth, Karl. *Church Dogmatics.* 3/3: *The Doctrine of Creation.* Edited by Geoffrey W. Bromiley and T. F. Torrance. Translated by Geoffrey W. Bromiley and R. J. Ehrlich. Edinburgh: T. & T. Clark, 1960.

———. *Prayer according to the Catechisms of the Reformation.* Translated by Sara F. Terrien. Philadelphia: Westminster, 1952.

Berry, Wendell. *The Gift of the Good Land: Further Essays Cultural and Agricultural.* San Francisco: North Point, 1981.

Brueggemann, Walter. "Pharaoah as Vassal: A Study of a Political Metaphor." *Catholic Biblical Quarterly* 57 (1995) 27–51.

———. *Praying the Psalms: Engaging Scripture and the Life of the Spirit.* 2nd ed. Eugene, OR: Cascade, 2007.

———. *The Spirituality of the Psalms.* Minneapolis: Fortress, 2002.

———. "'Theme' Revisited: Bread Again!" In *Reading from Right to Left: Essays on the Hebrew Bible in Honour of David J. A. Clines,* edited by J. Cheryl Exum and H. G. M. Williamson, 76–89. Journal for the Study of the Old Testament Supplements 373. London: T. & T. Clark, 2003.

Calvin, John. *Commentary on the Book of Psalms.* Vol. 2. Translated by James Anderson. Edinburgh: Calvin Translation Society, 1846.

Dempsey, Carol J., and Russell A. Butkus, eds. *All Creation Is Groaning: An Interdisciplinary Vision for Life in a Sacred Universe.* Collegeville, MN: Liturgical, 1999.

Forman, Kristen L., ed. *A New Century Hymnal Companion: A Guide to the Hymns.* Cleveland: Pilgrim, 1998.

Fretheim, Terence E. "The Plagues as Ecological Signs of Historical Disaster." *Journal of Biblical Literature* 110 (1991) 385–96.

Janzen, J. Gerald. "Metaphor and Reality in Hosea 11." *Semeia* 24 (1982) 7–44.

Kaufman, Gordon D. *Theological Imagination: Constructing the Concept of God.* Philadelphia: Westminster, 1981.

Kraus, Hans-Joachim. *Psalms 60–150.* Translated by John J. Scullion. Continental Commentaries. Minneapolis: Augsburg, 1989.

Lasch, Christopher. *The Culture of Narcissism: American Life in an Age of Diminishing Expectations.* New York: Norton, 1978.

Lifton, Robert J. *The Broken Connection: On Death and the Continuity of Life.* New York: Simon & Schuster, 1979.

Otto, Rudolf. *The Idea of the Holy: An Inquiry into the Non-Rational Factor in the Idea of the Divine and Its Relation to the Rational.* Translated by John W. Harvey. London: Oxford University Press, 1958.

Soelle, Dorothee. *Suffering.* Translated by Everett R. Kalin. Philadelphia: Fortress, 1975.

FURTHER READING

Brueggemann, Walter. *Awed to Heaven, Rooted in Earth: Prayers of Walter Brueggemann.* Edited by Edwin Searcy. Minneapolis: Fortress, 2003.
———. *Embracing the Transformation.* Edited by K. C. Hanson. Eugene, OR: Cascade, 2014.
———. *Hopeful Imagination: Prophetic Voices from Exile.* Philadelphia: Fortress, 1986.
———. *Into Your Hand: Confronting Good Friday.* Eugene, OR: Cascade, 2014.
———. *An Introduction to the Old Testament: The Canon and Christian Imagination.* 2nd ed. Louisville: Westminster John Knox, 2012.
———. *The Practice of Homefulness.* Edited by K. C. Hanson. Eugene, OR: Cascade, 2014.
———. *The Practice of Preaching an Emancipatory Word.* Minneapolis: Fortress, 2012.
———. *Prayers for a Privileged People.* Nashville: Abingdon, 2008.
———. *Praying the Psalms: Engaging Scripture and the Life of the Spirit.* 2nd ed. Eugene, OR: Cascade, 2007.
———. *The Prophetic Imagination.* 40th anniversary ed. Minneapolis: Fortress, 2018.
———. *Reality, Grief, Hope: Three Urgent Prophetic Tasks.* Grand Rapids: Eerdmans, 2014.
———. *Remember You Are Dust.* Edited by K. C. Hanson. Eugene, OR: Cascade, 2012.
———. *Sabbath as Resistance: Saying No to the Culture of Now.* Louisville: Westminster John Knox, 2012.
———. *Tenacious Solidarity: Biblical Provocations on Race, Religion, Climate, and the Economy.* Edited by Davis Hankins. Minneapolis: Fortress, 2018.
———. *Truth Speaks to Power: The Countercultural Nature of Scripture.* Louisville: Westminster John Knox, 2013.
———. *Truth-Telling as Subversive Obedience.* Eugene, OR: Cascade, 2011.
Brueggemann, Walter, with Carolyn J. Sharp. *Living Countertestimony: Conversations with Walter Brueggemann.* Louisville: Westminster John Knox, 2012.

Fretheim, Terence E. *Creation Untamed: The Bible, God, and Natural Disasters.* Grand Rapids: Baker Academic, 2010.

―――. *God and the World in the Old Testament: A Relational Theology of Creation.* Nashville: Abingdon, 2005.

Hankins, Davis. *The Book of Job and the Immanent Genesis of Transcendence.* Diaresis. Evanston, IL: Northwestern University Press, 2011.

Linafelt, Tod. *Surviving Lamentations: Catastrophe, Lament, and Protest in the Afterlife of a Biblical Book.* Chicago: University of Chicago Press, 2000.

Ward-Lev, Nahum. *The Liberating Path of the Hebrew Prophets: Then and Now.* Maryknoll, NY: Orbis, 2019.

SCRIPTURE INDEX